"Will's insightful book about running and the processes one goes through from being a standout athlete in the field to someone who has gracefully accepted slowing times is an inspiration to all of us aging runners. As someone whose best times are behind her, Will's book motivates me to get out the door and run and remember to smile and enjoy every mile, no matter how slow it is."

—Nancy Abraham; *Accomplished Northwest age-group runner and triathlete-finished 3rd in 2007 Triathlon World Championships in non-professional division.*

"There are certain people you meet in life and upon reflection, are almost scared how different your whole life could've been without having done so. A full-blown 'soccer kid', I thought distance running to be the silliest sport there was at first glance. My parents sent me to local road races in the beginning throughout Evanston to simply tire me out. Instead, no matter how hard I ran, I felt even more energized. Mr. Van Dyke was one of the very first to inquire about my progress after each race and it motivated me to have an improving answer for him throughout the years. Reading this book has me looking forward to another run together soon."

—Robert Gary; *Head men's track and field coach at The Ohio State University, 1991 State of Illinois 2-mile champion, United States Olympic team (steeplechase) 1996 and 2004.*

All the best - in life
and running !!

Will

RUNNING

COMMENTARY

A Life on the Run

Dane — Welcome to the
Evanston Running club —
Look forward to meeting you
on runs and at events.

WILL VAN DYKE

Will

Published by Galloping Gertie Press

ISBN: 978-0-615-58241-2

Book Design by Melissa C. Lucar, Fisheye Graphic Svcs, Chicago, IL

Cover Photo: Author finishing 10th in first Chicago Marathon in 1977.
Used with permission of *The Chicago Tribune*.

Photo Credits: p. 31, 32 Dr. Hugh Tatlock; p.34 *The State*, reprinted
with permission of the State Media Company; p. 22, 25 Larry and Nancy
Abramson; All other photographs by the author and his family

Printed in the United States of America

"Run Forever"

Bill Rodgers

"Running—I find myself in art"

Will Van Dyke
Six word biography

Dedication

This book is dedicated to my loving wife Johna, who was there at the beginning, to my son Garrett and daughter Gretchen, who have shared many miles with me, to grandsons Jack and Peter, and to son-in-law Dave Miller who has his own passion for running.

CONTENTS

Acknowledgements

First and foremost I want to thank my wife Johna for her first reading of these articles and her suggestions, and her patience and forbearance with a running husband. Thanks too to Lee Nagan and Melissa C. Lucar of Fisheye Graphic Services for helping make this book a reality and to Gary Wisby for editing the manuscript and offering his insight and to my daughter Gretchen, who offered her comments on the draft. Thanks to everyone in the Evanston Running Club who read these articles and whose many kind words gave me confidence that my words were affecting people, and a special thanks to all the unnamed people who have volunteered at races and events to make many of the experiences in this book possible.

Preface

This book would not exist were it not for the Evanston Running Club (ERC). I joined the ERC in 1974 and have been an active and inactive member, occasionally, ever since. Most of all I am indebted to the quarterly newsletter, without which, this book would never have been written. I started writing occasional articles for the newsletter in the mid-1990s. More recently I have been writing an article for each edition of the newsletter—winter, spring, summer and fall. Somehow before each edition of the newsletter was due, and article or the idea for an article would come to me, often while I was running, mind loosened up, free-associating as the miles went by and the ideas bubbled up to the surface of my brain. First I wrote one article, then another, until I had unintentionally assembled a small stack of articles. I usually got good feedback about the articles from other ERC members and my family. Nothing like positive feedback for motivation, is there? Armed with that feedback and the stack of articles, I began to consider the possibility of assembling them into a book. I had the title long before the idea for the book began. My minister, Barbara Pescan, who I often shared the articles with, coined the term, "Running Commentary," which, though not original, seemed like an excellent title for this book. I hope you enjoy reading the articles as much as I have enjoyed writing them. Blessings to all runners, fast and slow, and in between.

New Shoes—
From Converse All-Stars
to Asics

I just bought another pair of running shoes—Asics Gel, Roman numeral unknown—from a mail order company. The catalog had an overwhelming selection of shoes, but even with all the styles available, choosing a shoe was simple. I chose the shoes that most closely resembled the dark blue Tigers (now Asics) that I wore in the early 1970s. In between I've worn Nikes, Etonics, New Balance, Adidas, and even something called Lydiards (designed by Arthur Lydiard, famed coach of Olympic champion Peter Snell). But gradually over the years I've found that the Asics shoes best fit my running needs.

But what, you ask, did you wear before Tigers? Before Tigers there were my trusty Chuck Taylor Converse All-Star low-cut gym shoes. I wore them for training and for races in high school. I wore them training for college cross country, and I even wore them running my first marathon in Beltsville, Maryland, in February 1970. The amazing thing was not only that I ran in them, but that I ran a very respectable 2:52 marathon. I wonder what the world record is for a marathon run in gym shoes?

I wasn't the only one wearing Converse All-Stars back then, either. *Sports Illustrated* recently ran an article by Kareem Abdul Jabbar, reminiscing about his three NCAA basketball championships in the late 1960s/early 1970s at UCLA. The article had photos of Kareem (then Lew Alcindor) and his teammates. The entire UCLA team had on white Converse All-Stars with the Chuck Taylor emblem on the side. No Air Alcindors for Lew, just plain white high-top gym shoes, the same model I wore for running. Imagine how much better he would have been with Reebok Pumps, or a pair of Air Jordans.

But back to the Tigers. After finishing my first marathon I immediately entered the Boston Marathon. I knew my All-Stars weren't appropriate for a marathon as prestigious as Boston. I needed "real" running shoes. So while on a visit to

 Chicago (I was living in Virginia at the time), I went shopping for running shoes. Believe me, finding a pair of running shoes in 1970 was not as easy as it is in 1993. I finally settled for a pair of white and green Adidas Marathon shoes, though they were a half size too big. I guess the name clinched the deal for me. They were adequate for the race, but they had very little cushion and they gave me very large blisters by the end of the marathon.

After some experimentation with different types of shoes, I finally settled on my favorite—the blue Tigers with the white logo, nylon upper, no heel counter and the herringbone pattern on the bottom. I wore that type of shoe for many years and would probably continue to use them, if they were available. As my shoes have worn out, I've usually discarded them, but I kept one pair for sentimental reasons. They are the shoes I wore in 1973 when I finished 30th in the Boston Marathon. They occupy a shelf in my office now, but they're not blue. One year my wife, Johna, had them bronzed (they are actually silver) for me as a gift for my birthday. They serve as reminders of old friends from Boston, past races in New England and running to the peak of my ability.

April 1993

Still Running After All These Years

This fall marks the 40th anniversary of my running career. It began in fall 1961 when I tried out for the Timothy Christian High School cross country team. I was a senior and it was the first year our school, a member of the old Private School League, offered cross country as a sport. Before that in my sophomore year I had tried out and made the frosh-soph basketball team. Most of that time was spent on the bench watching other, taller, more talented classmates compete against rival schools like Chicago Christian, Walter Lutheran, North Shore Country Day School and Chicago Latin School. In my junior year, I had worked in an A&P grocery store and had not done any sports. When I tried out for the basketball team, I especially remember the running we did to get in shape before we were even allowed to touch a basketball. Oh how I loved running laps around the small school building in Cicero, Illinois. I was ecstatic just to be running. Our cross country coach, Leroy Prins, was also the basketball coach, and he knew less about the sport than we did. I would lead our group on five-mile runs through the streets of Cicero, urging everyone to keep up. We ran in high-top Converse All-Star gym shoes. Much to my surprise, and that of everyone else, I won my first race. My lungs burned and I coughed for two hours afterwards from the effort.

That spring I also participated in track and field. Since we had a very small school—there were only 42 kids in my graduating class—I not only ran the mile, but I also threw the shot put, did the long jump and ran the 100-yard dash, none particularly well. Even my times for the mile were quite pedestrian, usually about 5:30, but I had found a passion for running anyway.

Since that time, four decades have gone by and my running has ebbed and flowed, sometimes trickling into a dry streambed, when my energy was required for other, more important life changes. In the 1960s I devoured every book and article I could find about running and fitness. In those days running was an obscure sport, practiced mostly in the eastern states and California and here in Chicago at the University of Chicago Track Club. I still remember vividly the black and white format of *Runner's World* when it first came out, with the cover photograph of Jerry Lindgren (still holder of the high school 5000-meter record) after finishing a cross country race for Washington State University.

My college career was peripatetic, as I went from one school to another in search of self. At Calvin College, in Grand Rapids, Michigan, I was 7th or 8th man on a very talented group of runners, who won their conference and finished 10th in the country in the small school division. Often in dual meets I would finish ahead of the other team's first finisher. But sometimes I was almost the last man in the race. I remember one race in particular. We were running in an invitational meet on a golf course in Kalamazoo,

Michigan, at Western Michigan University, then NCAA cross country champion. I wound up running 58th out of about 60 runners in about 6 minutes a mile.

The next year I was a sophomore at Coe College in Cedar Rapids, Iowa, unable to compete at the varsity level because of NCAA rules. I ran with the freshman team but ran well enough to beat most of the varsity cross country runners. I ran many of the races barefoot, even on our home course, which was filled with oak trees and acorns. I think running barefoot connected me in some mystical way with my love of Native American lore and legends. As I ran, I could imagine myself an Ojibwa brave chasing deer through the forest in northern Minnesota.

After a year at Coe College, I dropped out of school for nine months to get my bearings, before resuming my studies at the Illinois Institute of Technology (IIT) on Chicago's south side in 1966. It was in that interlude that I met my wife Johna. At that time she lived with her parents in the Little Village neighborhood of Chicago (an area inhabited by a large Czech population), and I lived with my parents in Berwyn. Since we didn't have a car, we'd either borrow my father's car or ride the CTA on our dates. But instead of taking the CTA home after our dates, I'd often run the five miles home to Berwyn after saying goodnight, running through industrialized areas along Ogden Avenue and 31st Street in Chicago and Cicero. I still remember one evening in particular. It was well past midnight, and in Cicero I was stopped by the police. They couldn't imagine someone running for fitness at that hour, and my story about running home from my girlfriend's house must have seemed ludicrous to them, but they let me go nonetheless.

At IIT I was the sole member of the track team, running the mile in local meets at Elmhurst College and Concordia College, finishing as high as fourth in one meet in 4:38. I was self-coached, alternating runs of five to eight miles, with track workouts. I ran the track workouts on IIT's cinder track at 31st and State Street, a facility that has since been replaced with a building. I timed my workouts with a stopwatch used whenever I ran, on or off the track. Then later that fall I ran cross county as the lead runner on a mediocre team. I still remember my pride when Sonny Weisman, the athletic director, a former boxer, gave me a letter jacket with black leather sleeves and a red "I" on the front, even though I had only run one track season and one cross country season. These jackets were usually reserved for juniors and seniors who had proven themselves over their college careers. I was so proud, and I still cherish the jacket and even wear it occasionally.

At the end of the 1960s, while in the army at Fort Lee, Virginia, I ran my first marathon, in Beltsville, Maryland, a very respectable 2:52, good for 10th place. It was particularly astonishing, because prior to the race I had never run farther than 12 miles, either in training or in a race, and I ran the race in my trusty Converse All-Star low cut gym shoes, the same ones I wore in training every day. So from the 12-mile mark to the finish I was in unknown territory.

Then came the 1970s and, for me, amazing running success, especially in the early 70s when I lived with Johna in Somerville, Massachusetts, just at the border with Cambridge. The decade began with Patriot's Day 1970 when I ran my first Boston Marathon. There were a number things that made it memorable, not the least of which is that I was in the U.S. Army at the time, and I had my way paid to the race by the Army, because Jock Semple, the legendary race director, was kind enough to send me an invitation to the race after I had explained my situation. I wish I had kept that letter, but he basically congratulated me on my time from Beltsville and sent me an invitation, which I took to the Special Services representative on my base at Fort Lee, Virginia, and in the spring Johna and I drove north, from green, leafed-out trees in Virginia to cold barren leafless trees in Massachusetts.

Everyone who has run the Boston Marathon more than once has special feelings about the first race, and I do too. The day was cold. It rained the entire race with temperatures in the low 40s, but I was too excited to notice. I will never forget running through a gauntlet of screaming co-eds in Wellesley. The hair on the back of my neck stood on end. Then the runners ran through a narrow path with co-eds on both sides screaming loudly almost next to the runners. Now, when runners go through Wellesley, barricades on both sides of the road prevent the students from getting close to the runners. Equally exciting for me was my finish. I went into the Newton Hills in 100th place, and wound up an astonishing 94th in a time of 2:41, more than 12 minutes faster than the previous November in Maryland.

That spring we moved to Massachusetts, where we lived until 1974. It was in Boston that I truly became a distance runner. I joined the Cambridge Sports Union, an athletic group founded by Larry and Sara Mae Berman, who was one of the first women to run Boston. The intensity of my running increased dramatically. On Sundays I would do 20-mile runs starting out from Fresh Pond in Cambridge, running as far west as Waltham, often running on parts of the Boston Marathon course. Many days I ran home from work in Boston and then in Cambridge along the Charles River, running 80 to 90 miles a week and racing on weekends. During those years I raced in many of the old, established New England road races, running for the Cambridge Sports Union against runners from the North Medford Club and the Boston Athletic Association, usually finishing in the top three or four in races against some of New England's formidable distance runners, occasionally winning New England Amateur Athletic Union road races, and even finishing 2nd in a national 25k road race in Dedham, Massachusetts. In 1971 I had been regularly beating many of the better runners and I had high expectations going into the Boston Marathon and hopes of winning one of the coveted medals for the top 35 places. But, alas, I was far too excited and couldn't sleep for two nights before the race. I fell apart at the end and wound up finishing in 44th place with a time of 2:36. It wasn't until 1973 that I finally won a medal, finishing in 30th place with a time of 2:32!

One of my most memorable races, though, was as part of the Cambridge Sports Union cross country team in 1971 when we beat the feared Boston Athletic Association for the team prize. Our two teams had tied with the same number of points, but because our fifth man beat theirs, we won the championship. We were a ragtag group of runners, including me, an 800-meter runner from MIT, two high school runners, including the New England two-mile champion, and Larry Berman, founder of the CSU, and the old man of the group at age 37.

The latter part of the decade, the responsibilities of a young family reduced my running somewhat, but I was still able to train hard enough in 1977 to finish 10th in the first Mayor Daley Chicago Marathon, two weeks after the birth of Gretchen, our second child. Then in the late 1970s after starting graduate school, while working full-time, I had very little time or energy for running. I ran as much as I could, but days and weeks would pass, and I would not have run a step.

Then came the 1980s. I ran sporadically, occasionally racing on weekends. However, even in that decade there were entire years when I didn't run.

The decade of the '90s began positively. In 1993 I ran over 1,000 training miles and finished 7th in my age group in the CARA standings. I was looking forward to turning 50 in1994 and being the youngster in my new age group. But things didn't turn out that way. In early 1994 I entered a program of psychotherapy that lasted for five years. I only ran 48 miles the entire year. The next year I ran 500 miles, but in 1996 I didn't run a single step. This time the energy I had used for running was used to heal my fragile psyche of past wounds and old angers. I took time to grieve my losses, including the loss of my father, both the real loss from his death and the loss of the father I wished he had been. I mourned the loss of my son and daughter, as they left the nest and went away to college. Through therapy I was able to heal and to deal with these losses, both old and new. But the work of therapy did not leave me any energy for running. I did not run then, and I did not miss it. I could not run. Many weekend afternoons I just took very long naps as my psyche did the internal, hidden work of grieving and healing.

In 1998 I began running again, and this year I am recovering some of my passion for the sport. One of my favorite runs has always been the ten miles from my house at Asbury and Emerson up Prairie Avenue and up to Winnetka, around Indian Hill Country Club, and back again. I'm much slower now than when Clyde Baker and I used to run the same course in the 1970s and '80s, but I still look forward to running this route, which I have been running for over 25 years. Somehow being able to complete this run gives me deep satisfaction, even though I often struggle the last few miles, often stopping to walk occasionally to gather my strength before continuing on.

There are no marathons left in these legs, or in this heart, but I will continue to run for the joy and pleasure it brings me, knowing that down the road there will again be times when the energy I use for running may be needed elsewhere.

April 2001

Running with Clyde Baker

Next year I'll be 50 years old, a fact that amazes me, and makes me ponder, especially as I enter another age group and will be at the young end of an age group once again. As I consider my advancing age, my thoughts turn to my good friend and running partner, Clyde Baker, who had some of his best running times in his early 50s.

I first met Clyde in 1974 after we moved to Asbury Avenue in Evanston, just two blocks north of Clyde's house. We had just bought an old house that had formerly been known as "Sleepy Hollow" by neighbors and current and former Northwestern University football students. We were in the process of rehabilitating it and making it livable after the abuse and neglect it had received while being occupied by the former Northwestern students. One of Clyde's neighbors at the time, Robert Leeb, was a friend of ours and he told me that his neighbor (Clyde) was an internationally renowned soils engineer and also an accomplished runner. I don't remember exactly how we met. I think I called him. But in any case, that was the beginning of many long joyous miles running together.

We'd begin our runs from my house and travel north through Wilmette, through Kenilworth, Winnetka and Glencoe, and once in a while up to Lake-Cook Road in Highland Park and back again down Sheridan Road—a distance of 20 miles. Our favorite run was up Green Bay Road, across Central Street, up Prairie to Green Bay Road again, west on Kenilworth Avenue up to Ridge Road. Then we ran the two miles around Indian Hill Country Club and back home. The run is about nine miles long, or at least that is what I always put in my running log. Clyde, on the other hand, would mentally log 10 miles for the same run. Clyde would always add a mile or so to any distance I had estimated. I'd tend to underestimate the distance slightly, so I wouldn't give myself credit for miles I didn't think I had actually run. It got to be a joke with us. There was a "Baker 10" and a "Van Dyke 10." A "Baker 10" is not usually 10 miles, but somewhere between 8½ to 9½ miles, and a "Van Dyke 10" is 10 to 10½ miles, but never less than 10.

We would usually go for a short run of five to six miles on Saturday, and then on Sunday afternoon we'd do a long run of nine to 12 miles, or longer, if we were training for a marathon. The longer runs were my favorite. We'd always start out talking, catching up on work or family or political events. We'd also reminisce about past races we'd run. Clyde ran his first marathon at Boston in the 1950s while still an undergraduate at MIT, and I ran my first marathon in 1970, so we had lots to talk about. Than at some point in the run, usually past halfway, we'd stop talking and begin the serious business of training. What usually happened would be that one of us would pick up the pace. It would be imperceptible at first, but when one of us would speed up, the other would respond by keeping up the pace, and then pushing it up a notch. We didn't talk then (we couldn't), but we both kept pushing the edge until we were both in a groove, focused totally on our running.

In the late 1970s when Clyde and I were both in our prime, our runs were extremely fast-paced, especially the last two or three miles when we both smelled home. We'd often end up running our last miles at a pace well under six-minute miles. Depending on who was in better condition, the other would hang on for dear life, not wanting to lose contact. We'd finish our run, relax and drink some beer or juice at one of our houses and jog home for the relaxation and rejuvenation of a hot bath.

Clyde's achievements during the early part of his fifth decade were remarkable. He still holds some age group course records at several Chicago area races, including the Club North Shore Half Marathon. I too have ambitions of running well in my 50s, and I know most of Clyde's times will be out of my reach, but his achievements and effort and our training runs together will be my inspiration.

April 1993

Fond Memory of Jock Semple

It's February and the Boston Marathon is never far from my mind at this time of the year. I ran Boston for the first time in 1970, and had a memorable experience, thanks in part to Jock Semple. Many people remember Jock Semple as the Scotch curmudgeon who tried to prevent Katherine Switzer from running the Boston Marathon in 1967. He was viewed as a symbol of male chauvinism as he was caught on film trying to physically stop her from running the race which he viewed as the bastion of men only. His view was indicative of the times, when many men were trying to prevent women from doing things or entering fields that had historically been dominated by men. But he was one of the forces behind the Boston Marathon for many, many years with an office in the basement of the Boston Garden, home to the Boston Celtics.

From that office he processed entries to the race and organized other events for the Boston Athletic Club.

My memory of him is much more positive. In 1970 I was living in Petersburg, Virginia, as a PFC in the US Army. I was stationed there waiting to hear about my application to get out of the army as a conscientious objector. I had already been classified a non-combatant conscientious objector after being drafted, because of my belief in the immorality of war, and being totally against killing my fellow human beings. But that is another story. Anyway, the previous summer I had run several track races for Special Services, and then in December I ran a 12-mile race in the Washington, D.C. area in about six minutes a mile. That got me thinking about running a marathon, all 26 miles 385 yards. I found out there would be a marathon in Beltsville, Maryland, on the Washington Birthday Day holiday after consulting my latest issue of Runner's World. I entered the race and my wife Johna and I made the trek up to Maryland. Amazingly enough I ran 2:52 despite never having run over 12 miles. And that got me thinking about the Boston Marathon. THE BOSTON MARATHON!

I still don't know when I first heard about the Boston Marathon. In the late 1960s and early 1970s it wasn't the mega-event it is today. As late as 1966 there were fewer than 500 runners entered in the race. But I had known about it for a long time and had had the ambition to run it. This seemed like a perfect time to run it, and I decided to enter the race. 1970 was the year the Boston Marathon introduced qualifying standards. Before that time anyone could enter, but qualifying standards were introduced to limit the growing field, which started on a narrow street in Hopkinton. I had been aware of the standards prior to running the Beltsville race, but my time there was faster than the required qualifying time, so I was encouraged that this would be the year I would run Boston.

Before I prepared my application I talked to the head of Special Services on the base asking whether I could get the Army to pay my way to the race. He told me it wasn't a problem—I just had to get invited to the race! That seemed like an insurmountable obstacle to me. At that time most of the runners invited to the marathon had fast times, I mean very fast times, well under 2:20 I am sure. The race in 1970 was won by Ron Hill in 2:10, just to give you an idea of the type of runner who would have been invited. But I thought I would give it a try. I sent in for an application and filled it out with my time, and then I wrote a short letter to the BAA telling them of my plight, and asking them to invite me to run so I could get my expenses paid by the US Army. When I look back I think it was the height of hubris for me to even think I would be invited.

Several weeks later a letter arrived from the Boston Athletic Association. Inside was a letter signed by Jock Semple. He wrote congratulating me on my splendid times and offering me an invitation to run the 1970 edition of the BAA Boston Marathon. I was elated, and astounded, and took the letter to

Special Services to get authorization for my expenses to run the race.

That April Johna and I hopped in our 1963 VW bug and drove the 600-plus miles to Boston. We stayed with friends living in Cambridge to cut down on our expenses. On race day the temperature was about 41 degrees and it was raining, not a hard rain, but the kind of rain that makes one wonder why you chose to run 26 miles on that day. I lined up for the race in a dark blue sweat suit. But it wasn't just any sweat suit. It was a Christmas present from Johna. On Christmas we didn't have enough money for gas to drive to visit our family in Chicago, and we didn't have much money for presents either. Most were handmade gifts. I got Johna an antique rag doll for $3.00 at a shop in Petersburg, and she got me a sweat suit—the dark blue one I wore in the race. But

it wasn't just any sweat suit. Johna had customized it. On the back was a gigantic white peace symbol with a smaller one on the front.

So thanks to Jock Semple, the US Army paid my way to run the Boston Marathon, and I ran the 26.2 miles in my peace symbol sweat suit, finishing in 2:41, soaked to the skin and dripping wet at the finish line, but totally elated.

Jock Semple, wherever you are, thanks for the invitation to the run of a lifetime.

Postscript: That May I received an honorable discharge from the US Army as a conscientious objector and we moved to Boston. I went on to race with the Cambridge Sports Union in many, many road races in New England, often seeing Jock urging on the athletes of the competing Boston Athletic Club. In 1974 we moved from the Boston area to be closer to our family in Chicago with our newborn son, and I kept on running, even coming back a few Aprils to run Boston again.

February 2007

Skinny Raven Tee-Shirt

It was Saturday, February 22, and I was at my computer on the web following the women's Olympic Marathon Trials in Columbia, South Carolina. The web page was giving me written updates as the race progressed. No pictures, just words, like reading a story. It was frustrating, but there was no coverage anywhere else, not on the networks, or even ESPN. Can you imagine that? The women's Olympic Trials marathon race was not on television, nor was the men's marathon trials in May either. I couldn't believe it. I followed the race as it progressed, looking for the early favorites, Libbie Hickman and Anne Marie Lauck. But as the race developed, Christine Clark, the unknown woman from Alaska, was in third place at the 20-mile mark and she didn't give up. She moved into first place and won the race, qualifying for the Olympic Games in Sydney, Australia. What an incredible story! She trained all winter on a treadmill in Anchorage, Alaska, and won the Olympic Trials race on a very warm February day. She had improved her previous best time by almost seven minutes in the heat!

I kept reading the story on my computer screen, and then I saw the name of the club—The Skinny Raven Running Club. I saw the photo of her crossing the finish line wearing a singlet with the Skinny Raven Running Club emblem, a goofy-looking, jet-black raven with running shoes on its feet, inside a red circle with the words "Team Raven" above in large red letters. What a marvelous image! I was smitten. I had to have one of those! I wanted a Skinny Raven Running Club tee-shirt of my very own.

Well, how in the world does one get such a tee-shirt? Who could I call? On the Monday after the race, I called directory  assistance, and amazingly, to me anyway, I got the phone number for the Skinny Raven Running Store in Anchorage. That sure seemed like the place to begin. I called the store and someone answered. He said his name was John Clark. No relation, but it was Christine's coach! I congratulated him on the race, but he took none of the credit. "Christine is the one who did the work, she deserves the credit," he told me.

I asked if he had any tee-shirts with the logo, and he did. I couldn't contain myself. I bought five, one for my wife Johna, one each for my two grown children, Garrett and Gretchen, and one for Annie, Garrett's fiancée. They loved the shirts, especially Johna, because her favorite bird is the raven—the wise, irascible raven. Besides, we can wear them this summer, in Alaska, when we crew for the Alaska AIDS Vaccine bicycle ride between Fairbanks and Anchorage.

I love the shirt for what it represents too. Like Christine, many of us have made a breakthrough in our running. For me it happened in 1970 at the Boston Marathon when I improved my time by over 10 minutes and ran 2:41, placing in the top 100. I didn't qualify for the Olympic team, but it meant just as much to me.

I also love the shirt because no one else in Chicago will have one, at least for a while. I'm going to wear it to all my races this year, even though I will be running for the Evanston Running Club. Or as John Clark wrote in a note he sent with the shirts, "Wear with pride." And I will, and I will think of Christine and all of us who are running with a dream, hoping for a magical breakthrough.

April 2000

Running with My Children

Running with my two children, Garrett and Gretchen, is one of the deepest satisfactions of my life. They aren't really children; they are adults now, grown up and out of the nest. They left Evanston, where they grew up, to attend college and to test their wings after high school. Garrett went to Colorado to ski and hike in his beloved Rocky Mountains. Gretchen went to Tacoma and Seattle, and then east to Europe—to France, Italy and any point easily reached by train from Paris or Milan. But they always came back, and every time they are home, they come to me and say, "Dad, can we go for a run with you?" I am delighted, of course, to run with either of them and to share one of the abiding passions of my life.

Running has become one of the rituals we share when they come home. We usually run four or five miles, leaving from our house on Asbury Avenue, going either north or south, before turning to go east to the vast openness of sky and the ever-changing waters of Lake Michigan. Usually we do not talk very much while we run. We just run stride for stride, enjoying each other's company, sharing the sound of our feet on the pavement and the rhythm of our breath, in a kind of wordless connection and meditation, doing something we both love, being outdoors and moving our bodies.

Slap, slap, slap is the sound of our feet on the concrete sidewalks and asphalt streets. Scrunch, scrunch, and scrunch as we run along the crushed limestone path along the lake. That changes to a dull, muffled thud on the grass green carpet of Peter N. Jans golf course, near our house, until we run along the tree-lined North Shore Channel, through dry oak leaves that sound like crumpled paper under our feet. When we are about 200 yards from our house, they usually pick up the pace and sprint to the finish. I'm left behind, the victim of late middle age and declining fast-twitch fibers.

It wasn't always this way. Running was something I did, running almost every day when they grew up, occasionally running local races and even marathons. I never pushed either of them to run. Besides, they each had their own busy lives as children and then as teen-agers. Even though they didn't run, they were both involved in sports and physical activities. For Gretchen, it was figure skating and later in high school, soccer. For Garrett, it was soccer, lacrosse and skiing. In the late 1970s Garrett would often accompany me to cross country meets, when I coached the Illinois Institute of Technology cross country team. Occasionally we would run a local race, and they would run to stay in shape, but that was it.

That all changed when they began coming home from college during the summer and on breaks. They would ask to join me, when they saw I was going out for a run. We each looked forward to our time together. Last summer Garrett and I were coming back from a run on a warm August evening, tired but exhilarated from our run together. We hadn't talked much, but Garrett said to me, "You know, I feel like you let me in your church when I go running with you." He's right. Running has become much more for me than just a physical activity. It has evolved into a spiritual experience as well, a time when I am outside, feeling the heat and the cold and the rain, breathing in and breathing out, simply moving, in harmony with the earth and its rhythms, feeling complete. I am truly blessed to share this with the two of them.

August 2000

Intersecting Curves

Last August my 23-year old daughter, Gretchen, and I ran the Kemper Chicago 10k Classic through Washington Park, near the University of Chicago. She was home visiting us for two weeks between her summer job as a crew leader with Southwest Youth Corps in Durango, Colorado, and her return to Tacoma and the northwest, where she went to school. I look forward to her visits, however brief, and our runs together when she's home. After she arrived I told her about the race, and she jumped at the chance to join me.

On Sunday morning we drove to the race from Evanston, listening to *Satellite Sisters* on WBEZ, enjoying our time together. Since we were each going to run a different pace, we agreed ahead of time to meet at the bright yellow Vertel's Running Store tent. Since this was my first race of the year, I took off easy, being careful not to run too fast at the beginning. I was hoping to run seven minute miles, so I was pleased when I ran through the first mile in about 6:50, running well within myself. I tired noticeably at the end of the race, but still managed to finish under 44 minutes, or just over a seven-minute mile pace.

After finishing, I drank some Gatorade, and spent a few minutes recovering, before walking to the finish line to root for Gretchen when she finished. The clock at the finish said 50 minutes when I passed. I walked about 400 yards beyond the clock and waited, thinking she would finish soon. I expected her to come in between 50 and 54 minutes. I watched while the clock ticked off another minute, but still no Gretchen. Then another minute passed, and another. At 55 minutes I thought, "Poor Gretchen, she must be having a tough day." Then the clock reached 60 minutes, and I realized she had to have come by before 50 minutes. While I was drinking my Gatorade and recovering, she must have finished. I decided to go to the Vertel's Running Store tent, and yes indeed, there she was! "What time did you come in, Gretchen?" I asked. "48 minutes," she answered. No wonder I didn't see her finish, she was only four minutes behind me!

It made me realize that our running is marked by two different curves or trajectories. Hers is a descending curve with a downward slope. Her times will be decreasing as she gets older, but the arc of my curve has an upward sweep as I continue to slow down with age. For the time being my pace is faster than hers, but sometime in the future, and it's probably not too far away, our curves will intersect. For a time we'll be comfortable running the same pace, and will be able to run together in races. But after that, her curve will be below mine and she will run faster. Then she can wait for me at the finish line, but I hope she doesn't spend too much time recovering and getting refreshments, otherwise she'll miss seeing me finish too.

August 2001

Footsteps in the Snow

It was nine in the evening on Friday, March 16, the day before St. Patrick's Day, and I was outside running four miles in a snowstorm. My feet were making tracks as I ran, soon to be covered up with new fallen snow, erasing any sign that I had passed by. The calendar said it was almost spring, but winter was not about to go out without a fight. The wind was fierce from the north, biting at my face as I began running. For many people it was just a reminder that spring, and warmer weather, could not come soon enough. But I was actually enjoying myself, feeling the wind and the snow and the cold, plodding along through the snow, one of the few people outdoors. Everyone else was inside, probably nestled in front of a fire, watching a video, eating popcorn, but cursing the weather, wishing that winter would finally end.

For me, running through fresh snow in the spring is not the same as running through the snows of dark December, or even January, when winter's grip is still strong. In winter the days are short and the darkness seems overwhelming in its ferocity, creating, for me at least, a depression and a longing for the light that only comes later as the sun inevitably returns to warm our bodies. In winter the snow and darkness give no hint of leaving, and despair, not hope, hangs in the air. In spring the days are finally getting longer and the snow, though heavy and wet, will soon melt and disappear. Often, as on this night, the snow stuck to the ground and the sidewalks, but the street was only wet and slick, as the snow melted quickly on the asphalt. My spirit was buoyed, knowing this was only a temporary glitch before spring would return.

I was running one of the familiar routes from my house—a four-mile route that I know by heart. It's a route my feet have trod hundreds of times over the past 24 years. Up Ridge Avenue to Sheridan Road, then east to Lake Michigan, south down Sheridan, past the Evanston Lighthouse, out to the landfill at Northwestern University and then home down Emerson to Asbury Avenue. Sometimes I run fast, but usually lately I just run an easy pace, content to be running, feeling the wind and the weather, and simply enjoying the movement of my body.

On this night, as I ran south on the snow-covered sidewalk near Lighthouse Beach, I noticed other tracks. The footsteps were outlined crisp and sharp in the new fallen snow. They were fresh, made by someone running. They were too far apart to be those of a walker. They were the tracks of a solitary runner like me. Clearly I was not the only one who felt the need to run in the snow at nine o'clock on a Friday evening. I wondered about this person who had passed by just moments before. A person I did not see, but whose presence I felt. Was it a man or a woman? Was it a young person, or a middle-aged person? Was she running fast or slow, and why was she out running this late at night. I wanted to meet and share the experience. I wanted to say, "Isn't this fun, running in the snow, and isn't it beautiful out tonight."

Our paths crossed, but on another day or night, without the snow, there would have been no tracks on the sidewalk to make me aware of another person's presence. They made me appreciate another runner, a kindred spirit I did not see, but whose presence I had witnessed. I usually run alone, but this experience made me realize I am not alone, and that there are others who share my passion and who, too, can be exhilarated by running through the snow on a blustery March evening.

March 2001

On Not Running
the Chicago Marathon
in 2002

This year marks the 25th anniversary of the Chicago Marathon. Twenty-five years ago on September 25, 1977, marathoners made history running 26.2 miles through the streets of Chicago. I was there with them, making my own bit of personal history. Ten days after our daughter Gretchen was born, I ran the inaugural Chicago Marathon, then called the Mayor Daley Marathon (Richard J., not the current mayor, Richard M.).

Actually I didn't just run the marathon; I had a great day and made a personal record (PR). Even though I took off way too fast—I ran the first ten miles in about 56 minutes—I was able to hold on and finish in just under 2:33, good for tenth place. I was elated and felt like a winner. In fact I threw my arms up high and made two vees with my fingers as I crossed the finish line, as if I had won. And for me, I was as happy as if I had crossed the finish line first.

The next morning, I picked up the *Chicago Tribune* and went directly to the sports page to find the race results. I found the results, and yes indeed, I had finished 10th. There was even a photo on the back page of a runner crossing the finish line, with mud-splattered legs and back— in an Evanston Running Club singlet no less. It was me, with arms raised, looking for all the world like a winner! A *Chicago Tribune* photographer had captured the moment perfectly, and that's the photo you see on the cover of this book.

Since that time Gretchen has grown up, and we run together when she comes to visit us from her home in Seattle, or we go to visit her there. We even run races together occasionally, finishing separately, as we each run our own pace. Last fall she ran the Seattle half marathon the Sunday after Thanksgiving.

Late last year we decided to run this year's marathon after her success with the half marathon. We would run it together, crossing the finish line together. It made perfect sense. It was her 25th birthday on September 15, and the marathon's 25th anniversary on the 13th of October. It seemed like perfect symmetry combining the two. Unfortunately, my body didn't cooperate. Last year I ran more distance than I had in several years, and even ran a few races in respectable times. I was looking forward to finally running with her, instead of just running in the same race. But after running an excellent 8k at the Vertel Turkey Trot in Lincoln Park, things unraveled for me. My left knee became sore—too sore to run, so I took some time off. Then we sold our house and bought a condominium and the packing and the unpacking after the move didn't leave me with enough energy to run, even after the knee started feeling better. Since then I have been able to resume running, but not enough for the rigors of marathon training. Reluctantly, several months ago I told

Gretchen I just wouldn't be able to run the marathon with her. We were both very disappointed.

I had wanted this article to be a triumphant article about father and daughter running together in the Chicago Marathon with 37,500 other runners. Instead it is one of disappointment and an unrealized dream. But this November we're going out to Seattle to visit her over Thanksgiving weekend, and we're planning to run together in the Seattle half-marathon, unless my aging body once again intervenes. Keep your fingers crossed. I'll let you know how it goes in the December newsletter. Maybe I'll be able to show you a front-view photo of the two of us crossing the finish line, instead of a rear-view of a lone runner from long ago.

September 2002

Passing the Torch to Galloping Gertie

I just passed the running torch I have carried for over 40 years to my daughter, Gretchen, better known now as "Galloping Gertie." We ran the Seattle half marathon together on the Sunday after Thanksgiving. It was the first race we had ever run together and finished together. Many times before we had run in the same race with me finishing considerably ahead of her, but we planned this race to be different. We were originally going to celebrate her 25th birthday, and the 25th anniversary of my running the first Chicago Mayor Daley marathon, by running the Chicago marathon together, but my injuries and a move to a new condominium made the training impossible. So as an option, we decided to run the race in Seattle while my wife Johna and I were visiting Gretchen at her home in Tacoma, Washington, over the Thanksgiving weekend.

I should have known something was afoot when we went for a five-mile run on the Wednesday before Thanksgiving at Point Defiance Park in Tacoma. Point Defiance is a lovely park that overlooks Puget Sound with a road that snakes through large Douglas firs and other enormous trees. It feels like running through an enchanted forest. I half expected trolls and little gnomes to greet us as we ran. We parked the car at one end of the park near the zoo and began our run. Gretchen as usual took off much faster than I would have liked. Unlike her, I generally start my runs quite slowly, and then gradually increase the tempo near the end of the run, with a solid, hard finishing kick if I feel up to it. But Gretchen doesn't know the meaning of taking it easy. As usual she started out quite fast. She has always started out faster than me, but usually by the end of our runs together she would slow down. But not this time. As I struggled to keep up with her through the roads, and up and down the hills (yes, there were hills!) I realized she wasn't going to slow down this time, and I ran with her, but felt like I was running a race, not a training run.

It happened again two days later. We ran on a level stretch of park land along Puget Sound. I thought she'd run easy, just two days before the race, but we ran 4 miles at a pace well under 8 minutes a mile. She was ready!

Race day we got up early to drive to Seattle for the 7:30 a.m. start. The sky was absolutely clear! A blessing after four days of early morning fog. Over 7,000 runners assembled at the starting line near the Space Needle in Seattle. The first two or three miles were downhill. We struggled just to get through the crowd of runners, and then the walkers who had started 15 minutes earlier. We ran easily together watching the sun come up over Lake Washington, Gretchen ran just a little ahead as I tried to conserve my energy for the large hills I knew were coming at miles 9 or 10.

On the flat sections of the course we would usually run together. But whenever we reached a hill I would fall behind her. As a flatlander from Evanston, Illinois, my body was not ready for the hills. But Gretchen was. She would attack the hills, familiar to her from her runs up and down the ones near her house. I would plod up the hills and at the top she would wait for me to catch up with her. We did this for the entire run. It was clear to me that Gretchen was holding back a bit so we could run together. Near the end of the race there was a final steep downhill under a bridge and then a short but steep incline just before we entered the finish on the Astroturf in Memorial Stadium. I could barely make it to the top, my body spent, but there was Gretchen graciously waiting for me again so we could finish together, and we did, crossing the finish line holding hands as we had planned, finishing in one hour and 48 minutes. I cannot describe my feelings at that point. Joy for the run we had just shared, elation for finishing together, sadness at my own slowing, aging body, and just plain love and admiration for my daughter.

Two race volunteers wrapped us in protective Mylar blankets at the end of the race. We had our picture taken with two American flags as the backdrop, and then we climbed a set of stairs to meet my wife, Johna. We all hugged, and moist-eyed I told Gretchen that I was passing the torch to her, and it felt very good.

But why, you ask, the moniker "Galloping Gertie?" Gertie comes from her kindergarten teacher, who just called her Gertie. It was an affectionate name that our family and close friends have adopted for her. But after the race it was clear to me that she is not only Gertie, but Galloping Gertie. It really makes sense too considering that she lives in Tacoma, home of the original Galloping Gertie, a bridge near her house.

Galloping Gertie is a large suspension bridge across the Tacoma Narrows, the strait that separates Tacoma from Gig Harbor and the communities on the Olympic Peninsula. This is the second bridge constructed at that location. The first one was finished July 1940. It was supposed to be a technological wonder for the lightness and grace of its structure. But the engineers who designed it had pushed the technology too far. It was too light and lacked sufficient rigidity. Right after the bridge opened it started to sway in the wind. Locals started to call it Galloping Gertie because of this. Eventually the bridge collapsed, less than six months later, as strong winds buffeted and twisted the structure. You may have even seen it in old newsreels, as the pavement twisted in the wind like a towel blowing in a breeze, eventually twisting itself apart and falling into the water 200 feet below.

Well, Galloping Gertie sure seems an appropriate name for Gretchen now, and I gladly hand the torch to her. She has earned the right to carry it as she gallops toward her future with lightness and grace.

December 2002

Galloping Gertie Takes the Torch and Runs with It

I didn't run the Chicago Marathon this year, but I did something much, much better. I ran the last 10 miles of the race with my 26-year-old daughter, Gretchen, who was running her first marathon. What a thrill it was to share those last miles with her!

She's been living in the Seattle/Tacoma region for the past several years, since attending the University of Puget Sound. Two years ago on Thanksgiving weekend she ran the Seattle half marathon. I don't remember her exact time, but it was about 1:53 or so. Even then it occurred to me that she could easily break four hours if she decided to run a marathon. Then last year we ran the same race together in about 1:48 as she waited for me at the top of the many hills along the course. But the course took its toll on both of us, and her knees, like mine, were sore from the steep downhill parts of the course.

Last spring we were in Tacoma to celebrate the completion of her teaching certification program from the University of Washington. Her knees were getting better by then, and we ran together several times, and I made sure we ran on the flat course along the water, not up and down the hills near her house. As we ran, I marveled at how fit she had become. On one of her runs she announced that she was considering running a marathon in the fall, the Seattle Marathon. I gasped, but didn't say anything then. But I was concerned that she would damage her knees again on the hilly course. Later I told her she might think about running a marathon on a flat course, instead of the hilly Seattle course. Luckily, she too realized a flat course would be less of a strain on her knees, and she announced early this summer that she intended to enter the Chicago Marathon. I was relieved and looking forward to being her support crew for the race.

She began training in earnest during the summer and gradually worked up to a 20 mile run several weeks before the race. She called us right after that workout. "Guess what, dad," she said, "I just finished a 20 mile run in Point Defiance Park, and I ran eight minute miles." Eight-minute miles I thought. Oh my, this girl really is Galloping Gertie. I quickly did some rough calculations, and realized she should easily run 3:45. With some luck she could run 3:40 and even qualify to run the Boston Marathon.

I have run many marathons, including the first Chicago marathon in 1977, two weeks after Gretchen was born. I had always hoped that if she ever ran a marathon, we could run the race together, but I knew that would be impossible this year. Unfortunately I had been injured with plantar fasciitis, plus I had neither the desire, but much more important the training, to run a marathon. But I did think I could easily run the last five or six miles with her to offer encouragement and support for the most difficult part of the race. So that's the way we planned it.

A few days before the race I looked at a map of the course to figure out how to meet her at about the six-mile mark. I was hoping to ride the CTA to a Blue Line stop at about the six mile mark, but I was astonished to find that is the only CTA line that doesn't run on Sunday. So I looked for likely places to jump into the race, and the only one that seemed to work was at Greektown, just before they crossed the Eisenhower Expressway midway between Mile 16 and 17. So that's what we planned to do. It was farther than I had planned to run, but I thought I could keep up with her for about 10 miles if I had to, although I did have my doubts after hearing how well her training was going.

The day of the race was chaotic as you might expect, especially with all the streets closed in the downtown area. We dropped her off on Lake Shore Drive, said good-bye, and went off to park our car. We didn't see the start of the race, but we saw the thundering hoard come down State Street to turn west down Jackson. We continued walking west and we finally found an excellent spot to view the race from the railing of the bridge over the Chicago River on Jackson, right at the halfway mark. We got there before any of the runners arrived. Suddenly we heard a roar, and soon the first wheelchair racers came by to loud cheers. Then the front runners came through, the thoroughbreds, mostly Kenyans in their red singlets gliding effortlessly across the bridge, led by their pacer. At first the runners came by in small groups, but then the numbers swelled and they ran abreast, almost filling the bridge from rail to rail. Then, with the clock reading 1:50 or so, I spotted Gretchen running smoothly. We shouted encouragement as she ran by, and we proceeded west to Halsted Street to meet her.

I finally jumped in the race on Halsted Street when I saw her. I had to go from a dead stop to run at her pace which was about eight minutes a mile. She was glad to see me and I was just excited to be running. We talked together as we wound our way through the University of Illinois campus, then down Taylor Street, by the Illinois Medical District, through the Pilsen neighborhood and then Chinatown. The crowds were supportive, but Gretchen made sure they cheered when she came through. She raised her arms up and down urging the spectators to cheer, and they did. I was concerned about her expending all that extra energy, but her enthusiasm was infectious, and my concerns proved groundless.

We ran at a very steady comfortable pace. Gretchen told me she had crossed the start line at about the seven-minute mark. Even with that handicap, it seemed like she was well on her way to a good time. At the 20-mile mark she was on track for a sub-3:40 run, even with the seven-minute delay. I was getting excited and hoping she could continue to run strong.

When we ran through water stops, I'd get some water and Gatorade for myself, but I'd also get one or two extra cups of water to pour them over her head, or on the back of her neck to cool her off.

We ran down 35th Street through the IIT campus at mile 23, before finally heading south for the last three miles. Every time we ran by a mile marker it became clear that she would finish very close to a clock time of 3:40. I was so excited for her, and happy to be a part of it. By this time we had stopped talking and were both concentrating on running. I tried to run a bit ahead of her to give her something to focus on and to lead the way. Suddenly at about mile 24 I looked behind and there was Gretchen down on the ground. I looked and saw several stones on the ground. She must have tripped on one of them. Several nearby runners stopped to offer assistance. Luckily she got up and was okay and we continued our push to the finish.

We passed the 25th mile and continued south, finally turning on Roosevelt Road, but at that point she just stopped to walk up the incline to Columbus Drive and the finish. I could hear the minutes ticking away as she walked but knew she was just listening to her body. We got to the top of the hill and she turned down Columbus Drive again, running toward the finish. I had completed my mission so I slid off to the right, bent under the ropes of the police barricade, and disappeared into the crowd of spectators, while Gretchen ran toward the finish line, completing her first marathon. I saw that the clock was then reading about 3:38 and I knew that she would be very, very pleased.

When I finally met up with her and the rest of our group after the race, she told me that her corrected finish time was 3:32:26 and she had finished in the top five percent in her age group, and she had qualified to run the Boston Marathon. I was proud, of course, but most of all happy to have shared the last part of the race with her. Gretchen has indeed grabbed the torch I symbolically passed to her last year after we ran the Seattle half marathon. She has grabbed the torch and is off and running—no, she is galloping.

October 2003

The Healing Waters of Lake Michigan

For the past 18 months or so I have been injured—either injured or coming back from an injury. It all started in 2003 when I ran the last 10 miles of the Chicago Marathon with my daughter, Gretchen. I wasn't running very much at the time, but I was not going to miss the chance to run at least part of her first marathon with her. Especially since I had hoped that we would run the entire race together. That was not to be, so we agreed I would meet her with about six miles to go, but the six miles turned into ten. I was planning to meet her at the 20-mile mark when the race came through Chinatown by taking the CTA Blue Line there. That was before I found out there was no Sunday service to Chinatown. Instead I wound up meeting her at the corner of Halsted and Jackson in the Greektown, another older ethnic Chicago neighborhood, which was four miles farther from the finish line than I had intended. The ten miles went fine, the two of us clipping along at eight minute miles. Unfortunately for me, my longest run that year was about six miles, and several weeks later my left Achilles tendon started to hurt. It began hurting so much that it affected my running. I could still run, but the day or two after running five or six miles, I would limp noticeably and my tendons would be very sore. I started icing them after my runs to help the healing, but they were still very tender.

Then over Thanksgiving I got sick with a cold and I stopped running completely for a while, until after Christmas when I ran four miles, shuffling along is more like it, with Gretchen while she was visiting us over the holiday. That began a long slow recovery. After every run I would ice both my tendons. They would still hurt—even the next day while I walked to work, but somehow after two or three days off I was able to run relatively pain-free.

Spring came and once again I began running with the Evanston Running Club on their Monday night runs from Lee Street Beach in south Evanston. My tendons were still hurting, but it felt good to run with the group, and to feel the camaraderie and the energy of my fellow runners. Still the next day the tendon would be sore. Gradually as I built up my mileage the pain started to subside. I would ice the tendons religiously after every run. I started feeling so good by late April/early May that I decided to enter the Fox Valley 10-mile race in Elgin, a race I had run many times in the past, once finishing in sixth place in a time that now seems like it must have been run by another being—not me. I thought I would be able to run about 75 minutes. What an optimist. I ran just over 80 minutes, a personal worst (PW) by more than 5 minutes, but still good for third place in my age group.

But the hills in Elgin, especially going down, took their toll on my Achilles tendons. By mid-June I could barely walk without limping, but I kept on running. My tendons hurt when I ran, but the adrenaline of the runs made me forget about the pain. I just accepted that it would hurt a bit the day or two after a workout, but would heal enough to run in two or three days. Then, on one of the Monday-night runs in mid-June, I was about two miles from the finish, just south of the Evanston Lighthouse, and I just could not run anymore because of the pain. I had been running with Peter Elliot, and he saw me stop. I hobbled home through the Northwestern University campus, down Hinman Street to our condominium at Michigan and Lee Streets. As I got home the phone rang. I picked it up and it was Peter. He was calling to tell my wife, Johna, what had happened and that I would be home late. I guess I wasn't too late to answer the phone.

After that incident I stopped running again. I had no choice—my body had spoken and it was time to listen.

In early July we went on a week-long retreat with our church to Lake Geneva, Wisconsin and the former George Williams College campus. It's a lovely spot, but it is filled with hills, little ones and big ones that I limped up, and down, for the entire week. Johna thought I had become an old man the way I shuffled along. At that point I would have been grateful just to be able to walk without pain or limping, let alone run.

After we came home from that trip I started to ride my bicycle instead of running just to be doing some cardiovascular exercise. I would go for long 15-mile rides on the weekends and shorter ones once or twice a week. Gradually my tendons began getting better. Finally in mid-August I started running again, just a little at first. I remember how elated I was when I could run four miles without feeling pain. It was still summer so I began ending my run at Lee Street Beach, just two blocks from our home, and wading into Lake Michigan to cool off. At that time the water temperature was in the 60s—tolerable but cold enough that I didn't have any desire to wade further than the mid-calf. I found that the cool water made my tendons feel much better, so I continued doing it all through the fall and early winter. As the water got colder and colder, I found I could only tolerate a short stay in the icy waters, but the cold seemed to be helping my tendons heal.

It became part of my running routine. At the end of my run I would slowly walk the boardwalk at Lee Street Beach to the water's edge, take off my shoes, and wade slowly into the water up to mid-calf. My stay varied depending on the season and the temperature of the water. I found that I looked forward to it. I kept doing it until early December, even on my evening runs, when it was dark and I was the only one on the beach. There is something very peaceful and serene about being on the beach, even in the dark, and feeling the cold water numb your feet and ankles. It has evolved into a spiritual practice as well, giving me time to reflect on my run, embrace the wonder of the place where the land, the water and sky meet, and have the cool healing waters embrace my tired tendons and muscles.

I haven't waded in the water since last December, but the days are getting longer, the ice is almost gone from the shore, and I look forward to wading into the healing waters of Lake Michigan again to soothe my body—and my soul.

March 2005

The Last Lap

Doris Brown Heritage just ran her last lap on a track in Washington in late May. I read about it on the Internet in an article from the *Seattle Times*. The photograph in the article showed her beginning her last mile on the track in West Seattle, accompanied by 200 of her friends and runners she had coached at Seattle Pacific University for the past 30-plus years. At age 62 she was running that mile to mark the passing from runner to non-runner, because on the next day she was scheduled to have hip replacement surgery that would leave her unable to continue her lifelong love affair with running.

So who was Doris Brown Heritage anyway? I remember vaguely knowing about her as a young man, but I was not really aware of her accomplishments until I recently read some of the articles about her exploits and her amazing running career. How many of you are aware of her amazing career and accomplishments? She is the Joan Benoit Samuelson of the 1960s, a pioneering American woman long-distance runner, who ran in the days before the running boom, without the hype and fanfare, before *Runner's World*. She is the first woman elected to the National Distance Running Hall of Fame.

She ran in an era when women weren't supposed to be able to run long distances. In 1968 she made the United States Olympic team at 800 meters, the longest event allowed for women. Can you believe it? I am incredulous as I write it, that before that time 400 meters was the longest distance allowed for women. But for Doris, the distance runner, 800 meters was too short. Even so she still finished fifth in the 1968 Olympics in a time of 2:03.9 behind Madeline Manning, who tied the world record in 2:00.9. She made the Olympic team again in 1972, when the women's 1,500- meter run was added. But fate was not with her. She injured her ankle just before the race was to begin.

As a 16-year-old she set the American women's record for 440 yards. In 1966 she ran an indoor mile in 4:52 to set the world record, the first time a sub-5:00 minute mile had ever been run indoors by a woman. In 1967 she won the first women's international cross country championship in Wales, leaving the rest of the world's runners in her wake. She went on to win five consecutive championships in that event—an amazing feat in any age.

Equally important for her has been her coaching and mentoring young runners. For the past 39 years she has coached track and cross country at Seattle Pacific University, with her athletes earning national recognition.

But what I am most struck by is how much she loved to run, especially through her beloved West Seattle area, where she ran through woods, near the water, occasionally seeing bald eagles overhead, or hearing sea lions barking along the shore. Here's what she has said about her running:

"I think the aesthetics are what I love most about running. A love of nature. There's a lot going on by the water. Even when I ran cross country, it was the elements I enjoyed. The mud and the rain and the hills. Many of us are drawn to what we enjoyed as a child. For me it was the feeling of being at one with nature. I hate to call it endorphins, but there's a feeling when you put yourself on the edge of your comfort zone (that) this is very important." Who of us has not felt, if not expressed, similar sentiments.

So it was with a touch of sadness that I read the article. Sadness for one of our own, someone special, but a runner just like you and me, not being able to do what she loves to do—what we as runners all love. But there was also for me an understanding of the gift that running had given her, and that she had given to running, and that she will continue to give through her coaching and her inspirational career.

June 2004

Wake Up and Smell the Coffee

Wake up and smell the coffee! It's a phrase my mother repeated to me often when I was a child. In my mind I have a mental image of a cream colored-coffee mug just like the one I use every morning, with steam drifting from the top, swirling in the  air. She usually said it to me because I wasn't paying attention, or was lost in my own world, dreaming as I often did, and still do, about nothing in particular when I should have been listening. Actually I'm still very much that same kind of person, only now I'm much older, but still a weaver of dreams and daydreams. For me that's where the writing comes from, that place of dreams and daydreams. That's also the source for much of my creativity.

But it can be disconcerting sometimes, and potentially harmful. Like the time I was riding my bike as a youngster on a side street in Berwyn, in one of my reveries. Suddenly I had ridden my ten-speed bike right into the back of a parked car. Thud! Luckily for me it was parked and not moving.

Fortunately I found running, or it found me, and now I have a socially acceptable place to daydream. On the run I can daydream to my heart's content, and no one even knows. The irony is that running looks just the opposite of a dream-like activity. It looks like a totally focused, linear activity, with a clear objective and a goal. Instead, while I run, my mind drifts, and ideas and thoughts float gently through my brain and back out again, like clouds moving, drifting and changing shape continually. Often, after running three or four miles, I don't even remember where I have been or where I have run, as the thoughts and ideas randomly come and go. There is something about the unfocused energy of the run that loosens and unlocks ideas, and opens up a creative channel. The ideas for this article, and most of the articles I have written for the Evanston Running Club newsletter, came to me on the run. After the run it's my task to take the germ of an idea and elaborate on it. When my brother-in-law died, the tribute I gave at his memorial coalesced on a run, a run of grief and healing, after being with our family reminiscing about his life.

I suspect too that I'm not the only runner who daydreams on the run, or uses running as creative nourishment. In fact, the writer Julia Cameron in her books on creativity suggests that walking, which I interpret to include running, "is the most powerful creative tool I know." I couldn't agree more.

So if you see me, or I see you, out running along Sheridan Road, or up Green Bay Road, or through Gillson Park, lost in a dreamy reverie, let's not forget to offer each other a cup of coffee.

February 2002

Personal Worst—or The Hare Becomes the Tortoise

PR—Personal Record. That's what motivates many of us runners. PR—running the fastest ever for a given distance. We all want to do that, don't we? Greg, our fearless Evanston Running Club president, urges us to e-mail him with our race results, especially the PRs after a weekend of racing to let him and other ERC club members know about our accomplishments. What wonderful satisfaction we get after such a race, particularly when we have been trying for a long time to better a previous record we set, often getting close, but just missing the mark. "Guess what," we announce with childlike delight, "I just ran faster than I ever did before" for that race, for that distance—whether it's a mile race or a marathon. Then the feat gets duly noted with a postscript

"PR" after the race and time so everyone can share the knowledge of one of our runners setting a personal record.

Unfortunately for me, the days of PRs are long past. I am now in the brave new world of the dreaded "PW"—Personal Worst. It has been happening regularly the past few years, and it keeps getting worse. I don't race much anymore, but it seems each time I race the time is slower than the time I raced before. Last year it was the Fox Valley 10-mile run, which I have run several times in the past, finishing in the high single digits, and running under 54 minutes. But last year I decided to run it even though I was running less than 20 miles a week, maybe more like 15. "Hey, what the heck," I said to myself, "I should be able to run 75 minutes." Maybe I could even catch up with Nancy Rollins, one of our own ERC members and one of the premier masters runners in the United States. How foolish I was! I started out slowly, hoping to begin pushing the pace at about five miles. Ha—at five miles I was already fading fast, and by the time I crossed the finish line my time was just over 80 minutes, more than 30 minutes slower than my best 10 mile race. Another PW! It didn't even help when I found out later I had been first in my age group—60 to 65 years old. No, it was another PW and I just slogged through the last five miles with not even the glimmer of a fast finish on the mile-long downhill to the finish. The rest of the year was beset with plantar fasciitis and other assorted ailments and I didn't race again.

I began this year running free from the lingering injuries of the past year, and I was hoping to race more until I went for my annual physical in February only to be told by my primary care physician that my prostate gland didn't feel quite right. He said, "It's probably nothing, but you should have a biopsy just to check it out." The biopsy showed that I did indeed have prostate cancer—very early stage and curable. After getting educated about the disease and our options, we decided that surgery was our best option, but since the tumor was slow-growing we didn't need to rush. We decided to schedule the surgery for early May. But before the surgery I thought I would run the 8k Shamrock Shuffle on April 3. Before the race I once again had visions of catching Nancy Rollins down the backstretch, but reality quickly set in when the race began, and once again I had another PW. When I looked at the race photos on the Internet I couldn't believe what I saw. There it was in full color. No hiding, as I shuffled to the finish line on my way to another slow, tortoise-like time.

I had my surgery about a month later and it was successful. After a month off, I resumed running again in early June. The first day back I ran a slow, slow two miles, but it felt so good to be running after my recovery, and in mid-June I was back on Monday night running along the Lake Michigan shoreline with my fellow ERC club members. Then I remembered about the Wilmette Fourth of July four-mile race, a race I had won many, many years ago when it was six miles long and went west of the Metra tracks through downtown Wilmette. Hey, another chance for a PW, and I didn't disappoint, coming in well over 30 minutes, but not too bad considering I had surgery just two months before, and I even walked for about 100 yards at the three mile-mark to catch a short rest. Greg, our cheerleading president, was at the finish offering encouragement to the ERC runners. I talked to him at the end of the race when I was exhausted and just feeling tired from the effort. He tried to cheer me up, but all I could think of was how slowly I had run. But the next day I looked on the Web for the results and was surprised to see that I had won my age group. I was ready to take whatever encouragement I could after having set yet another PW.

Lately I've had a bit of time to reflect, and even though I will probably be setting more and more PWs in the next few years, at least I am able to run for now without any major injuries. Plus I have survived cancer surgery, and for that I am very grateful. So I will continue to plod along, going not so gracefully, or willingly, from hare to tortoise, on my way to another PW.

July 2005

40 Years of Running
with *Runner's World*

I just got my new *Runner's World* in the mail and was pleasantly surprised to see "40th Anniversary Special" emblazoned on the front cover. Forty years—can it be I have been reading the magazine for that long? I knew I had been running that long, but I didn't realize I had been reading the magazine that long. Not only have I been reading the magazine that long, but I have been subscribing for almost that long as well.

Until last year I had been faithfully keeping the old issues in the storage locker of our condominium, a stack that was about three feet high, dating back from the early 1970s through the 1980s. If you look on page 71 of this month's issue you will see a picture of Gerry Lindgren (*the* Gerry Lindgren!) shaking hands with Mike Ryan after a cross country race. That issue, from 1970, was in my collection, along with others with equally memorable covers. We had moved them four years ago when we sold our house and bought the condo. Before moving we ruthlessly culled our possessions, getting rid of many things we had been keeping just because we had unlimited storage space in our old house on Asbury Avenue. But I just couldn't part with those magazines. Every time I looked at them was a trip down memory lane with the photos of past Olympic champions on the cover, seeing a young Gerry Lindgren again and reliving races and scenes from long ago. So they came with us to the new space, with a single storage locker smaller than most of the closets in our old house.

Gradually I began to realize I really wasn't going to re-read the magazines, was I? They were in the storage locker because I just wasn't ready to let them go. But then we started looking at our storage locker and realizing there were still items in there we were never going to use, but that we couldn't part with, so we began getting rid of more stuff. The magazines weighed on me. I couldn't part with them, but I thought they might be of interest to someone else. Why, they might even be worth something. So I looked on e-Bay, but without any success. Then I sent an e-mail to Evanston Running Club members hoping someone would be interested in having them. But again there were no takers. I was stymied.

But then Dave Miller came into my life. He is the marathon-running boyfriend of our daughter Gretchen. He is a running maniac, running marathon after marathon, as well as many shorter races. He actually reminds me a lot of myself when I was his age in my late 20s and 30s, running race after race, although I must say he runs races that I would never have thought about running, like trail runs in Washington State traversing several thousand feet of elevation change. Last summer the three of us had a wonderful time running together on Vashon Island just off Seattle and Tacoma in Puget Sound. We'd start together but inevitably we would finish well behind Dave as he went into gears we were not capable of.

Dave and Gretchen came to visit last Christmas. Knowing that he is an avid reader, lover of history and student of running, I gave him my *Runner's World* collection for Christmas. Now they reside in their apartment in Tacoma. I hope he enjoys them and wonder where they will eventually wind up after he has looked though and read them.

Postscript: Not only have I been subscribing to *Runner's World* for most of its 40 years, but sometime in the early 1970s my mother-in-law gave me a subscription. But it was no ordinary yearly subscription—it was a lifetime subscription. Yes, they were offering lifetime subscriptions for $75 at that time. I suspect no one in their actuarial department knew of the offer, especially to such a healthy sub-group as runners. That subscription even survived the turbulent 1980s when the magazine was sold to Rodale Press, which is the current owner. So far the subscription has paid handsome dividends with race results, training articles and a sense of running history over the past 40 years. Not only that, but at my current age I have gotten one heck of a bargain. It's less than 20 cents per issue for the subscription so far, and I'm hoping to get that down to ten cents before one of us expires.

August 2006

Blazing New Trails on Overlapping Paths

This has been quite a year of change for Johna and me. We have just moved from our house in Evanston at 1847/49 Asbury Avenue, where we have lived since 1974. It is a wonderful Victorian house filled with memories of our children growing up and the life we created there. I have run from that house many thousands of times, mostly north through Wilmette, Kenilworth and Winnetka. Many years ago, when I was training for marathons, I would run as far north as Glencoe, to Lake-Cook Road, the dividing line between Cook County and Lake County, a 20-mile round trip from the corner of Asbury and Emerson.

When we first moved to Evanston I bought a United States Geological Survey Map, the kind with contours that hikers and backpackers use to plan their trips. Using that map I plotted the distances from our house, and I developed almost all the routes I would use over the next 28 years. I had a route for almost every distance between three miles and twenty miles. There was the four-mile route to the south, down Asbury to Main Street, east to Lake Michigan, north along the lake to Sheridan Road and back west to our house. The five-mile route went south to South Boulevard, and then east to Sheridan Road. But most of the routes took me north along Green Bay Road to Prairie Avenue and then farther north. My six-mile route, the one I have taken most often—maybe as many as 1,000 times in the past 28 years-took me east to Plaza del Lago in Wilmette and then south along the cobbled brick streets of Wilmette. One of my favorite parts of that run is the segment through Gillson Park. There I saw the lake in the summer with the beach full of bathers or heard the surf pounding in the spring and fall. I saw it in the dead of winter, when I was the only person in the park and the beach was piled high with windblown ice and snow. I have watched the winter sun glow red-orange as it set over Peter N. Jans Golf Course while I ran up the slight incline in the park past the Coast Guard Station. It is there one evening, just at dusk, that a red fox darted out in front of me just as I entered the north end of the park by the water filtration plant. That is the first, and only time, I have ever seen one of these elusive animals.

My favorite route was a nine or ten-mile run that I ran countless times with Clyde Baker—a long-time Evanston Running Club member, who still holds the national 30k record for 53-year olds—when he and I were both in our prime in the 1970s. It goes through Indian Hill Country Club in Winnetka. There is a two-mile-long road through the country club that loops around the golf course. I still don't remember how I found out about this road. The entrance is on Ridge Road, and it looks quite private and foreboding. Clearly they weren't encouraging interlopers like me to go into the grounds, but I did, and it was lovely and quiet with houses on the left and the open space of the golf course on the right as we ran clockwise through it. Clyde and I used to be the only ones who had discovered it for running. However, in the 28 years that I have been running others have discovered it too—runners, joggers, walkers and bicyclists. Often we would leave the country club and extend the run to 12 or 14 miles by continuing north to Cherry Street or Tower Road in Winnetka, before turning south on Sheridan Road for one of our blistering runs back home.

In the intervening years my appetite for long runs and marathons has vanished. I've been running less and less, and not doing many of the longer runs. Last year I managed several runs through Indian Hill Country Club, but this year injuries and the energy required for moving have severely curtailed my running. The move to our new condominium has also required that I create new routes for my runs. All I've needed this time is a map of the City of Evanston to plan my routes. We now live at Michigan Avenue and Lee Street; far enough south in Evanston that running along the lake from Lee Street Beach to Lighthouse Beach and back again is five miles. If I stretch the distance and run north to Sheridan Road, or Isabella—the dividing line between Evanston and Wilmette—that would be a six-mile round trip—which is about the current limit of my runs. So it looks like I'll be spending my time running in Evanston, along the lake and through the Northwestern campus. I will be content, but I will miss many of my old haunts up north.

July 2002

Embracing the Night

I got off the train two weeks ago at the Main Street Metra station at my normal time and looked west from the station. I was startled to see a glimmer of light on the horizon with touches of pink and orange in the fading sunset. The sky was not the usual inky darkness of December and January that I have become accustomed to. But as I walked home, I was once again blanketed in the darkness. After I got home, I changed into my running clothes and went out the door into the same blackness that had prevailed since just before Halloween when Daylight Savings Time began.

Accustomed as I am to running at night in the late fall and winter months, I hadn't thought a lot about the subtleties of darkness. Dark is dark, right? Well, not really. One night recently I realized there are many gradations and varieties to the night and the dark. It reminded me of the Inuit native people, who are thought to have many hundreds of names for the snow. Those names came from a very close observation of, and familiarity with, winter snow and white. Like the Inuit people I was becoming to know darkness in detail, the opposite of the whiteness they live in.

Some nights when I run through the parks along Lake Michigan I can barely see the white limestone path in front of my feet. On those nights it is indeed dark. The words "pitch black" come to mind. I proceed cautiously, because I have nearly run into other runners coming toward me out of the blackness. Bicyclists are especially dangerous because of their high speed. I'm always grateful for the riders who have headlights or other lights to warn me of their presence. But on other nights, when the clouds are low, the night sky glows pink with reflected light from Chicago and the other communities in the metropolitan area. Then I can clearly see the path stretch in front of me, and if I look south I can clearly see the silhouettes of the leafless trees with their winter branches exposed.

Then of course there is the moonlight. When the moon is full, or nearly so, I often stop running at Lighthouse Beach Park and go to the bluff overlooking Lake Michigan, transfixed, looking east or south, to watch the moonbeams as they dance and sparkle on the water.

My favorite nighttime running comes on a clear night after a light dusting of snow has fallen. Then the darkness disappears, and the sky glows and sparkles with reflected light from the snow.

The winter darkness will soon give way to increased daylight. It won't be too long before the ERC Monday night runs begin again. You'd think I would be looking forward to running in the early evening light after so many months running in the dark. But part of me enjoys my solitary journeys under cover of darkness, sampling the many moods of the night and subtleties of the dark. I find I actually wish the darkness could continue a bit longer before giving way to the inevitability of spring light.

February 2003

Red Moon Rising Over Lake Michigan

During the week I usually run in the evening, after 9 p.m. It just seems to fit my schedule. Usually I'm too tired to run when I come home from work. I come home, have dinner with my wife, Johna, do a crossword puzzle together and relax. Then, later in the evening, three or four times a week, I go out for a run of three or four miles. Usually I take a part of my run along Lake Michigan going north between Lee Street Beach and Clark Street Beach.

This past October I went out for my usual run. It was dark and cool. The darkness enveloped me as I ran, and the lights from the houses created a warm glow in the windows like lanterns illuminating the darkness. As I ran, I imagined families snug at home, warm in their houses, reading books, watching television, playing on their computers or putting their children to bed.

I reached the lake and I was the only one there. Not a soul was outside and I had the lake to myself, despite living in Evanston, a city with 80,000 people. Then out of the corner of my eye I thought I saw a red glow. I did see something red, red-orange! At Lee Street I stopped to look out into the blackness, and there it was. The moon! But not just any moon. A waxing, almost full, red ball of fire, rising in the east at 9:30 in the evening. I stopped running, transfixed by the sight. I could not take my eyes off the moon as it rose. It was magical, glowing and shimmering on the horizon.

As I watched in awe, I wondered why people weren't coming out of their houses to see the moon rise. Running out of their houses to see the spectacular display. This most amazing sight. Why was I the only one watching? Why weren't others coming out of their houses? Why weren't they shutting off the lights in their houses to better see outside? I wanted to hear someone say, "Martha, look, look! You have to come and look. Quick, get the kids!" The more I watched silently alone in the darkness, the more I expected people to come out of their houses, shouting. I could visualize crowds of people standing along the beach, clapping and cheering, yelling, "Bravo! Bravissimo!" as the moon rose. But no one came out to join me. I was the solitary witness at Lee Street Beach.

After a time I began my run again, thankful I had seen the moon rise, as wonderful and miraculous as any fireworks display. An event, so common, but still awesome in its beauty, like sunrises and snowflakes, rainbows, and red leaves in the fall. Or, as Johna, would say, "Just an ordinary miracle." An ordinary miracle that made me realize I don't run just for the exercise, but to experience moments like that.

November 1999

Running and Painting

Running and painting. Now there's an unlikely combination, you say, but not for me. I do them both, run and paint watercolors, but lately I find that I am painting more and running less and less. It wasn't something that I consciously set out to do, but it has been a gradual evolution. Last fall I had three watercolor paintings in a show sponsored by the North Shore Art League. Entry into the exhibit was almost as easy as entering a race—no qualifying time, no jury to convince—just pay the entry fee. So I paid my $20 membership dues, and as a member of the NSAL, I was entitled to exhibit three paintings in the show. That was fortuitous, because at the time I only had three finished paintings worth exhibiting. Much to my surprise, when I went to pick up the paintings at the end of the show, I had a note from a woman asking me whether I would be interested in exhibiting my paintings of barns in a real converted barn/restaurant in Batavia, Illinois. I asked how many paintings she needed. "Oh, there is space for around 20 pieces," she said. Twenty pieces, I gasped! Fortunately for me she said I could share the exhibit with another artist, reducing the number of pieces to ten, still seven more than my then current output.

Toward the end of last year I did my painting in my art class on Fridays and ran my usual three days a week. After running the Seattle half marathon last November with my daughter, I remained consistent in my training, running about 15 miles a week. I was looking forward to spring and Monday evening runs with the Evanston Running Club. But a trip to St. Louis to visit my two-year-old grandson, Jack, changed that. When we visited Jack he had a cold. We shared hugs and kisses, but we also shared his germs. We both caught a cold from him, first my wife, Johna, and then me. At first I didn't run because I was sick, but then I didn't because I was concentrating on my watercolor painting, preparing for a show in early June.

Instead of running I painted, but mostly I did the work of preparing for the show—getting the paintings framed, getting them professionally photographed, and creating a mailing list. Then I coordinated with Brian DeWolf, the photographer I am sharing the show with, to prepare a postcard for the show. I never realized there was so much work having a small exhibition. All the time I was doing this I really didn't miss running, and then as I reflected on it, realized that the painting actually springs from the same creative source as running. No wonder I didn't miss it. For me, at least, I think running has as much to do with creativity and expression as it does with athletics and fitness. It is about movement and grace: it is about joy, the sheer exuberant joy of self-expression. When I run alone there is no audience, but as I run mile after mile, I feel a connection with other creative souls, especially dancers, whose art is graceful, lyrical movement.

When I began running over 40 years ago in high school, it was not just about running. Running seemed to fulfill some need from deep inside. What I mean is that running connected me with the memory of the child in me that loved to run, leap and play exuberantly, just for its own sake. Look at any playground; you'll see what I mean. Painting has been a parallel path for me, but it has had a very long gestation period. I remember, before starting high school at a small private school in Cicero, Illinois, wishing I could go to the public school and study art, which they didn't offer at my school. That wasn't to be then, but now I am painting, expressing my creativity in a different form, just as I have done with running.

I will run again, but for now I am enjoying painting as my new creative path, wondering where it will take me.

If you want to see the results and the wonderful photographs of the Fox River Valley by Brian DeWolf, the show opening is on Saturday, June 7, from 1-4 p.m. at the Bistro, a bar and restaurant in Batavia, Illinois. If you miss the opening and somehow wander out to the Fox River Valley, it will be up for two months after that.

Postscript: The show is up and gone, but since that time I have exhibited again at the North Shore Art League and sold two paintings. I've even had enough time to run occasionally with the ERC on the Monday night runs.

April 2003

Running with Thanks
and Gratitude

Recently I heard Garrison Keillor say that we should begin every day with a sense of gratitude, and I do. Often when I run, I find that the rhythm of my feet slapping against the pavement—plop, plop, plop-—has become a meditation, a prayer if you will. As my two feet hit the ground, first one, then the other, I say "Thank....you." Thank you to no one in particular, but thank you. Thank you for the gift of this day, for being able to run, to feel the air caress my skin, to see the sunset over Peter N. Jans Golf Course, to smell the breeze off Lake Michigan as I run in the park along the lake. I give thanks for all of that, and so much more. Thanks for my wife of 37 years, Johna, and her love and support. Thanks that both my grown children, Garrett and Gretchen, are healthy, thriving young adults. Thanks for my daughter-in-law Annie and my grandchildren, Jack and now Peter, born three months ago. Each footfall is a prayer of thanks.

Someone, I'm not sure who, has said there are only two prayers—"Thank you" and "Help me." I feel fortunate now that my prayers are all thank you, although I know that there will come times when I will again need to ask for help, but for now my life is blessed.

Lighthouse Beach in Evanston is the midpoint on my usual five-mile route north from our condominium. In the past year or so I have begun to stop my run there at the gate to the lighthouse keeper's house, and walk through the white picket fence, through the Jens Jensen wildflower garden to the crest of the dune overlooking the lake. There I pause briefly, often with my hands clasped together, and I look out over the lake. I take in the smell and the wondrous sight of the lake. Often I run in the evening and just look out into the blackness, the infinite mystery of existence, and I say a brief prayer, giving thanks for the people in my life, sometimes asking for guidance or help. Then I resume my run, refreshed with profound gratefulness.

In a recent sermon at my church our minister, Reverend Barbara Pescan, read a meditation by Ralph Waldo Emerson that captures so much better than I can this idea of prayer and meditation.

"Prayer is the contemplation of the facts of life from the highest point of view. It is the soliloquy of a beholding and jubilant spirit.
Now, may you pause and see the wind
Remember the winter
Be witness to the flight of the birds
And look upon your own inner facts of life
From the highest point of view."

That is what I do when I pause, mid-run, at the crest of the dune, and I suspect that many of you do the same, in different ways as you run feeling the same sense of awe and thankfulness for your life.

March 2004

I Love Monday

I love Monday—Evanston Running Club's Monday night runs, that is. During the dead of winter when the winds are howling off Lake Michigan, and snow and sleet slam against my cheeks, I ache for the long days of spring and summer and our runs on Monday nights from Lee Street Beach in Evanston to Baha'i Temple in Wilmette. It's the time of year when I emerge from the dark days of winter and solitary runs along the lake to a social running experience. It's a social time for me because I don't run the indoor track workouts with the club in the winter, and until this year, I haven't participated in the Wednesday evening track workouts at Evanston High School. So when spring comes again, I can join with fellow runners for a lively run, camaraderie and conversation.

This year has been particularly rewarding because I found a group who were running at about the same pace that I do—somewhere around eight minute miles, more or less. The pace was usually slower, but very often faster, especially when we made the turnaround at Gillson Park to retrace our steps back south to our beginning at Lee Street. In past years I have been frustrated with the Monday night runs because I was a "tweener"—too slow to keep up with the faster runners, and too fast for the slower runners. So on many nights I found myself running solo, wondering why I even bothered to show up, since I was running alone anyway.

But as I said, this year was different. We'd all start out together, but then by the time we reached the Northwestern University campus we would be sorted into our respective groups. Phillip Martinez, Geoff Brodhead, Tim Guimond, Erik Walter, and others would be the leading the way, but not too far behind I would be running in a second pack with Garry Shumaker, Erika Vazquez and one or two other runners. My idea of a good run is to start out easy, warming up for a few miles, and then get into a good steady rhythm for the rest of the run, running hard the last mile or two if I feel good. But early in the year it seemed like most of the runners in our group had just the opposite strategy. They would run hard at the beginning of the run, and then hang on or drop off the pace after the Gillson Park turnaround.

That was extremely frustrating for me because starting out fast meant I was running at close to my race pace at the beginning of the run, and then hanging on for dear life and exhaustion on the way back. My motto, learned from famed New Zealand coach Arthur Lydiard, was "Train, don't strain." That is, a training run is just that, a training run and not a race, but somehow Monday nights seemed to bring out the competitor in everyone. It became a test to see who could keep up, or not. Each week when my pack of runners would start out fast, I would repeat my mantra, "Train, don't strain," and gradually it seemed to sink in. Garry, Erika and I would start out a bit slower than usual, make the turn at Gillson

Park, and then we would get serious. Gradually Garry fell back as Erika would pick up the pace. I would respond by staying even with her and then she would pick it up again, and I would strain to hold on, hoping she didn't decide to run any faster, and eagerly looking forward to reaching the gravel path again south of the university, knowing we only had one more mile to the finish. It went like that week after week in the summer. Garry, who had started out in early summer about to keep up for about two-thirds of the run, gradually got stronger with more endurance, and each week he would run with the two of us farther and farther past the turnaround, first staying with us to the Evanston Lighthouse, then to the City of Evanston Water Filtration Plant and then to the gravel path. Each of us I think enjoyed the rhythm of our runs, running side by side, stride for stride, pushing each other. We all became better runners last summer, in part, because of our Monday night runs together. Erika improved the most, lowering her half-marathon time from 1:45 last year, to 1:31 this year. Garry didn't race much, but he clearly has gotten fitter this year, and I had one of my best years for a long while, mostly because I was fit and injury free.

Then, as it does every year, summer began to draw to a close. Each week, darkness came earlier and earlier, until it was almost dark when we started our runs in October. With the end of Daylight Savings Time the first week in November the 2008 season of Monday night runs was over. Darkness and the cold will force a change of venue to SPAC where runners can stay warm and dry inside waiting for everyone to arrive, and this year the day will be changed to Wednesday, at least for a while. I will continue to run on Monday evenings though, starting not from Lee Street Beach but from my condominium three short blocks from the beach. Bring on the darkness, the cold and the rain, until spring comes again. But this winter I won't always be running solo. Garry, Phillip and I have been continuing to run together on Monday evening, and Erika expects to join us, when she recovers from her knee injury. You are welcome to join us any Monday if you want. Most of all, I'll be counting the days to spring, and meeting at Lee Street Beach for our weekly forays to Baha'i Temple and back.

November 2009

Running on Vashon Island— Team Van Dyke's First Race

My family and I just spent two weeks in Washington on Vashon Island in Puget Sound, a short ferry ride from either Tacoma or Seattle. We rented a house on the beach where we relaxed and watched the tide come in and go out in a lovely rhythmic lunar dance, leaving behind sand dollars, crab shells and jellyfish. Every day a bald eagle perched nearby on a large pole sticking up through the water about 100 yards from the house. Two herons came to the shore daily to fish and hang around, and seals bobbed up and down in the distance. But the best part was spending time with our family. Our daughter Gretchen and her boyfriend Dave Miller live nearby in Tacoma, and they stayed with us. Our son Garrett and his wife Annie and his family also came, and we got to spend lots of time with our grandsons, seven year old Jack and three year old Peter.

The two boys played on the beach, swam and combed through piles of driftwood looking for sticks suitable for their games. What is it about young boys and sticks? Jack and Peter had swordfights and gun battles with their driftwood finds. Jack found one stick that he carried around with him constantly, using it as a bat to practice his baseball swing. He was devastated when it broke, convinced there was no replacement, even though there were dozens of similar sticks nearby.

Vashon Island is about the size of the island of Manhattan, with a population of only 10,000 people. It is rural, with a very small city center with a four way stop sign and a flashing red light above, and not a single traffic signal. I ran a lot while on the island, by myself and with Gretchen, Garrett and Dave. It's a beautiful place to run, but "Oy the hills," especially for a flatlander from the Midwest like me. I tried to find running routes along the shoreline where it's flat, but there is just no place to run on the island that is flat for any appreciable distance. No, there is always a hill to climb, and then another, and then another after that. Needless to say, my quadriceps muscles got stronger after all those hills, but often I had to walk several times before reaching the top of a hill.

There was a Strawberry Festival on the island the second weekend we were there. They didn't have many strawberries for sale, because the festival was started many years ago when they actually grew them on the island. But there was a parade through the downtown, and a race, the 27th annual Bill Burby Fun Run to honor the man who was the founder of the race. Once we found out about the race it seemed destined to happen. Gretchen had originally wanted us to run a 5k over the new Tacoma Narrows Bridge, built next to the bridge that was once called "Galloping Gertie," which was to open that weekend. It would be a first and only run, since once the bridge opened to automobile traffic it wouldn't ever again be closed for a run. That race also seemed appropriate for Gretchen, since she is our own "Galloping Gertie", but we decided on the island race. Besides once you are on the island, you just don't want to leave, and running the bridge race would have meant leaving the island for much of the day. Plus the price was right for the Bill Burby run, only ten dollars. When was the last time you ran a race for ten dollars, and got a new t-shirt to boot? So we decided to run the race. The three Van Dykes opted for the 5k and Dave for the 10k.

Remember the hills? The race started at the local YMCA, then ran downhill for almost two miles to about sea level, before heading back up to the finish at the Y. The downhill was just terrific. I was cruising. At about the midway point I was following a runner who looked to be in my age bracket, with grey hair and a beard. He had been ahead of me for quite a while but I finally caught up with him after one of the long downhill stretches of the race. Ha, I thought I should be able to beat this guy. But then I began the slog back up the hill, and it became clear that he was a local, used to the hilly terrain, and I was but a flatland pretender soon to get shown a thing or two about hill running. He soon pulled away from me, beating me by about 20 seconds. I came in at about 24:30, or more than two minutes seconds slower than I had run in the recent Ricky Birdsong race in Evanston on a flat course. I ran the last mile in 10 minutes after running near seven minutes for the first two miles. Gretchen came in the second woman after leading for about half the race. Garrett came in a couple of minutes after me, and Dave came in 10th in

the 10k, but unfortunately he is in the very competitive and fast 30-39 year age group, and he was fifth in that group. We all had a great time. It was the first time all of us had run together like that, and I look forward to this fall when we will all be running the LaSalle Bank Chicago Marathon together for another first.

What a treat to be sharing one of the passions in my life with my family. The enterprise that started out as one solitary long distance runner, namely me, has now expanded to four of us, what I call team Van Dyke/Miller consisting of me, Garrett, Gretchen and Dave Miller.

But we haven't stopped growing, I suspect. I expect that number to increase soon to five. Jack, our seven-year-old soccer kicking, baseball playing grandson, was at the race on Vashon enjoying the festive atmosphere and watching earnestly with his grandmother Johna and younger brother Peter as all of the runners approached the finish line. He first saw Gretchen come in, then me, then his dad, and finally Dave who had run the 10k. He told his Dad that he wants to run a race too when he goes home to St. Louis. What a treat that will be for him, and us. Maybe all five of us can run a race together in the near future. When Jack joins us, we'll have a team of five, our very own Van Dyke-Miller cross country team. I can't wait.

July 2007

Marathon Swan Song

It started last Christmas in Lake Geneva, Wisconsin at the house our family was renting for the holiday. It dawned on me that this year would be the 30th anniversary of the Chicago Marathon, a race I had first run 30 years earlier in the inaugural Mayor Daley (Richard J, not Richard M, although it seems like Richard M's been mayor of Chicago that long) Marathon. Five years earlier I had run the last 10 miles of the Chicago Marathon with our daughter, Gretchen. I had wanted to run the entire race, but I was injured at the time and marathon training was out of the question. But this time I wanted to run the entire race with her. There was certain symmetry to the 30th anniversary since she was born two weeks before I ran the first one. I also decided it would be my last marathon—my swan song—having run close to 20 marathons since 1969.

As we talked about it, our son Garrett, who is four years older than Gretchen said he'd like to join us in his first attempt at the 26.2 mile distance. Gretchen's boyfriend, Dave, was a shoo-in to join us. He's an official marathon maniac, the actual name of a group of Northwest runners who like to see how many marathons they can run in a year. It's an elite running club for the truly addicted among us.

So we made our plans for the race. I registered all four of us early, made plane reservations for Gretchen and Dave to come from Tacoma, and we took the first steps on our road to the starting line on October 7, the date of the race.

The race this year dovetailed with my involvement with a local Evanston charity, the Ted Fund, which gives three year scholarships to disadvantaged third, fourth and fifth grade students to attend the summer camp of their choice. While searching the LaSalle Bank Chicago Marathon web site, I found out that non-profit charity groups can sign up to have runners raise money for the charity, if they have the required number of people sign up to run for their charity. More importantly, I found out that we could sign up for the event and be an official charity with as few as 15 runners. Well, we already had four, so we were on our way. The question was, "where were we going to get the other 11 runners, or walkers, to meet our quota?" I brought up the idea of the charity at the next Ted Fund board meeting soon after. Two of Ted's sisters and his mother enthusiastically agreed to sign up and walk the marathon to raise money.

At that point I was only hoping to get 15 runners signed up so we could meet the minimum charity requirement. I was less concerned with whether they were actually going to help raise funds, because without 15 runners, we couldn't even qualify as a charity. Then I enlisted Evanston Running Club runners with an e-mail announcement and an announcement at our Monday night runs. After making the announcement, I remember Tim Guimond asking me during the run, "Who is this Ted guy anyway and why is he so important?" I was a bit startled at his reaction, but I explained the origin and mission of the Ted Fund, and Tim later signed up and was a very effective fund raiser for the organization. With my cajoling and people's generosity, we eventually had 15 runners sign up, and we had made our quota to become an official charity of the Chicago Marathon.

Then came the bonus entries. Being named an official charity carried with it a specific number of bonus entries, with the number dependent on the total number of charity entries. Bonus entries permit runners who missed the official deadline (this year reached in mid-April when 40,000 runners had signed up) to enter the race if they agreed to raise money for one of the charities. Once the deadline passed, e-mails started coming fast and furiously, as predicted by the fund raising coordinator, from people who wanted to run, but missed the sign up deadline. We could add up to five additional runners who agreed to raise money for the Ted Fund. Five additional runners eventually signed up.

Then came the hard part: training to run 26.2 miles. I hadn't run a marathon since 1993 when I last ran the Boston Marathon. I knew it wouldn't be easy starting from a base of less than 25 miles a week. I figured that a gradual build-up in my long run from 10 miles to 20 miles would get my total weekly mileage to 35 to 40 miles, which would be adequate for the distance. Training proved much harder than I thought, especially during the extremely hot weather we had this summer. Most of my long runs were a slog, alternating between running and walking, with more walking than I ever would have imagined possible. If it was difficult for me, it was doubly so for Garrett training in St. Louis. You think it's hot in Chicago? Imagine spending a couple of days trying to run when the temperature is 101 degrees and the humidity is 90 percent, not to mention the hills, which are non-existent in the flatlands of Chicago.

Meanwhile in the Pacific Northwest, Gretchen's training was going much better. She's a teacher, and she spent much of her summer training to do a half iron man (woman?) in Spokane, which she eventually did in splendid fashion, finishing second in her age group. Dave was just the energizer bunny churning out week after week of 60- or 70-mile weeks with at least one 20-mile runs every week.

Meanwhile the fund raising didn't seem to get going until late in the summer. I had set a modest goal of raising $6,000. I figured we might get 10 runners to actually raise money at $600 each. As the fund raising coordinator I would get e-mails every time someone made an on-line donation. I still remember my excitement when we reached $1,000, then $2,000 and then over $3,000. The money was mounting up. I had secretly hoped we would raise $10,000, but kept that to myself. When we passed $6,000, I was elated, and when we got to $10,000 I was ecstatic. The runners eventually raised over $13,000, more than double my initial estimate.

Prior to the marathon, we watched the weather reports religiously to see what the conditions would be on the day of the race. It became obvious late in the week that record heat was predicted. Not a good omen. Then, the week before the marathon, Dave called me to let me know he wouldn't be able to run the race. The marathon maniac had had a nagging injury of his shin that had been diagnosed as a stress fracture. There would be no Chicago Marathon for Dave this year. But Dave's misfortune would eventually work out to benefit the three of us so we could all start the race together.

When we signed up for the marathon each of us had been assigned to a start location, or corral, based on our recent marathon times. Dave, who had recently broken three hours, was to start up front in Corral A, and Gretchen was not far back in Corral B. Garrett and I were consigned to the Open Corral, way in the back, which meant it would be many minutes before we crossed the starting line.

I had been hoping to start the race with Gretchen, in honor of the 30th marathon anniversary and her 30th birthday. But I hadn't run a marathon in over 15 years, and hadn't run a fast race in many, many years, so I didn't have a recent fast time to qualify for one of the premium stating corrals. I did have an alternative plan. I wrote a letter to the director requesting to be assigned to the B Corral with Gretchen, explaining that I had run the first Chicago Marathon 30 years before (noting that I had finished 10th) and asking for a special dispensation to start the race together. Graciously, and thankfully, they honored my request and assigned me to Corral B. Two down, one to go. Now how could we get Garrett to start with us too?

The Saturday before the race we went to the marathon expo to get our race numbers and goodie bags. Dave got his too, even though he wouldn't be running. Then Garrett had a wonderful idea. Put Dave's number, with Corral A in bold letters, over his own number before the race. That way the three of us could start together, knowing full well we wouldn't be finishing together. On race day we were side by side in Corral B when the gun went off. Gretchen took off, as we knew she would. Garrett went out ahead of me, as I started out very conservatively considering the heat, and my relative lack of training.

For me, the race was a slog. Despite starting out conservatively, I found myself running with the 3:40 pace group, a group I thought was a reasonable target on a cool day, but not today. At about the 10 mile mark I began an inevitable slowing, not so much a slowing actually, as alternating between running and walking, then running for short periods between long periods of walking. I stopped at every aid station to drink Gatorade and water. I poured water over my head and down my back to try cooling off, but it didn't help. I'd shuffle on for a few hundred yards, and then resume walking. I hope to permanently delete the photos of the race. I am in total denial that the person walking in the photos was me—not a chance. I eventually finished in 5:08, more than double my time of 30 years before. Garrett finished about 10 minutes behind. When we eventually found Gretchen at Buckingham Fountain after the race we found out that she had finished in 3:37, slower than her previous marathon, but a terrific effort considering the conditions and still fast enough to qualify for the Boston Marathon, a goal that eluded many experienced runners that awful day.

So much for a marathon swan song. According to Wikipedia, the phrase «swan song» is a reference to an ancient belief that the Mute Swan (*Cygnus olor*) is completely mute during its lifetime, except for singing a single, heartbreakingly beautiful song just before it dies. Instead, this was a clunker, more like

a belly flop, than a swan dive, or anything beautiful related to a swan. But I am completely satisfied. I got to start the race with my two children, and I am so proud of each of them in their own way—Gretchen for carrying the torch of my passion

The Running Van Dykes, and Dave Miller before the 2007 Chicago Marathon

for running and Garrett for taking on the challenge and finishing the race, despite the horrible conditions.

Finally, I am so pleased that we were able to use the marathon to raise a significant amount of money for a charity that is near and dear to my heart. Thanks to all the Evanston Running Club members who participated in the endeavor with us—by running the race, soliciting donations, or just letting us use their entry to help get us to the minimum number of charity entries. It was a total team effort.

November 2007

Running Free—
Without a Watch

We runners are obsessed with time, aren't we? What was your time? How fast did you run that last mile? What was your time last year in the 5k, or the 10k, or the marathon? What were your split times? Time to speed up, or we'll never break three hours, or four hours or five hours, or whatever your goal is for that day, or that year. We obsessively time ourselves, don't we, not just in races but in our workouts, and our daily runs. We become disappointed when we run a particular distance slower today than we ran it yesterday, or last week, or last year.

What is your image of the start of a race? Mine is of lean, fit bodies crouched forward, ready to spring into action, finger ready to press the button to start their stop watches. The start of Chicago, Boston or New York, or any local race is always the same.

Runners poised, finger ready. Why do the elite runners do it? I can understand the guy in the back of the back, because he or she won't cross the starting line until well after the elite runners begin their races. In any elite marathon there is a clock stationed every mile to let runners know their elapsed time. What is that about? At the finish line the clock is prominently displayed showing the time, and each runner will likely have access to a photograph showing the time when they crossed the finish line, as well as the splits along the way if the race is is chip timed.

We're not just obsessed about time when we race, either. Most of the runners I know measure themselves daily against the clock, feeling elated when they run a particular workout faster than the time before, but disappointed when it's slower. I see that obsession in our Monday night runs from Lee Street Beach in Evanston. These runs should be training runs. Remember Arthur Lydiard's admonition, "Train, don't strain." Instead they often turn into "beat the clock" runs to see if last Monday's time can be bettered.

One Monday night I was running with a very accomplished young woman, a recent graduate of the University of Wisconsin Platteville, I believe, who had run a half-marathon well below 1:30. As we were running together I noticed a beeping sound every two minutes or so, and then she would look down at her watch. After a while it started to get on my nerves, disturbing what was an otherwise peaceful run at a good solid pace. When I finally asked her what the sound was, she told me her watch was giving her the split time every quarter mile. Every quarter mile! Not only was it a watch, but it had a GPS system, so she knew her time at whatever distance interval she wanted. What possible benefit would it be to know your pace at such frequent intervals? What if she was running too slowly? Did she then have to speed up for the next quarter mile?

This obsession with time is natural to us runners though, isn't it? It's how we measure our progress, but often to the detriment of enjoying our runs, listening to our bodies and the rhythm of our shoes slapping the pavement, feeling the wind, and the rain and the snow as we run. This fall Garry Shumaker and I ran together most Saturdays, running eight to nine miles. Our route took us through the Northwestern University campus where we ran though Deering Meadow along Sheridan Road just west of Deering Library. I don't remember any of our times, but I do remember the maple tree in the northeast corner of the meadow near the library glowing, bright red orange, in the setting afternoon sun.

When I first started running over forty years ago I carried a stopwatch with me on every run. Not a stopwatch on my wrist, but an old-fashioned stop watch, with a glass crystal face and a sweeping second hand that I held in the palm of my hand. It was a present from my wife, Johna. I timed every run and wrote the time down in my running log book after each run. Gradually over the years the obsession with time evolved into a love of the untimed run. Oh, I still run hard some of the time, and I can tell a hard run from an easy run, but I don't know how long it took. I think all of us develop a sense of what is a slow pace, and a moderate pace and a fast pace. We know when we are running too fast. Running without a watch allows us to run free, without the restriction of time, able to enjoy each run and what the day brings without being a slave to the watch. Some days when I start out I feel sluggish and tired. Sometimes that feeling subsides after a mile or two and I am refreshed, ready to have a solid run. Other days the spirit is with me and I feel frisky from start to finish. But however I feel, I enjoy that day, grateful not to be a slave to the stopwatch. If you don't already, why not try leaving the watch at home for some of your runs. I guarantee you'll enjoy it.

March 2009

Team Van Dyke
Has a Great Weekend

Our eight-year-old grandson, Jack, is a third grader at Edgar Road School in Webster, Missouri, nicknamed the Jaguars. He loves sports, and much to the chagrin of his father, Garrett, he loves the St. Louis Cardinals. In May, his school had a fundraising event for the athletic department consisting of a 5k race and a one-mile race for kids and adults. After that there was a 100-yard dash for the children with a separate race for each grade, beginning with the kindergartners and finishing with the fifth graders. For the kids the real fun would begin after the races with rides, food, games and other festivities.

We go to St. Louis frequently to visit Jack and his five-year-old brother Peter, so we decided to visit them the week of the race. I decided to run the 5k with my son Garrett. I assumed Jack would run the one mile event, with Peter, but I was oh so wrong. Jack, who plays soccer, and loves to run, decided to run the 5k along with many of his friends. Peter and his "grammy", Johna, would do the one mile. Afterwards the two boys would run the 100 yard dash with their respective age groups.

The St. Louis area can be unmercifully hot even in May, but on the Sunday morning of the race the temperatures were in the high 50s, and I was relieved. We started out in the semicircular driveway at the school entrance. Jack and one of his buddies sprinted from the start in a flash. He was 400 yards ahead of me before I knew what had happened. I didn't catch up to them until almost one mile into the race as I ran my steady seven minute miles. The two of them looked like they had no intention of slowing down. The race had lots of twists and turns through the residential neighborhood around the school—twists and turns, and the unavoidable hills, which are everywhere in the St. Louis area. Toward the end of the race it seemed like I was near the finish line, but there was one more turn, before I finished in the driveway where we had started with a time of 23:20—not great but okay.

Garrett didn't catch up with Jack until almost two miles into the race. He finished in a tad over 26 minutes. Then Jack came in, sprinting to the finish in 28:20, a good time for an eight year old boy by any measure, especially when we found out later than the course was a bit long. My guess is that it was more than a tenth of a mile long. As the finishers came in, I was amazed at the number of Jack's classmates who had run the 5k, which is quite an accomplishment at any age, isn't it? I suspect in the years to come

I'll be catching up with Jack later and later in the 5k race, until one day, he waits for me and his dad at the finish line.

Peter and Johna did the mile together, sort of. Peter would run ahead, then look back and wave and then go back to his grandmother, or wait for her to catch up. They finished together in around 20 minutes.

Then the real races began—the 100-yard dash in the school driveway. The kindergarteners took off first, running as fast as they could to the finish. I watched admiringly as each class raced to the finish, noting with special delight how fast the young girls were running. In grades K through 4, there was usually a young girl in the top three.

But then the fifth graders went to the line. They were off, running far faster than the younger children, but this time there were two or three girls in the lead. The two top finishers in the race were girls this time, not boys. What I noticed in all those young children, both the boys and the girls, was how joyful they were as they raced all out to the finish. All the children joined in and had a good time.

Seeing the young girls running made me think back to the not-so-distant past when young women's opportunities for running, especially distance running, were very limited. It wasn't until 1928 that women were allowed to compete in the Olympic Games. Did you know that in the 1960 Olympic Games, the longest women's race was 800 meters? The women's 800 race was eliminated from the Olympics in 1928 when several women collapsed at the finish line. Women were thought to be too frail to run that far. The 5k wasn't added to the Olympics until 1996, replacing the 3,000-meter race, and the 10k wasn't added until 1988. The women's marathon wasn't added until 1984. Who can forget seeing Joan Benoit Samuelson winning the first women's Olympic Marathon in Los Angeles? I know I can't. I still get goosebumps remembering her early move to get to the lead that helped propel her to the win, and then seeing her enter the Olympic Stadium alone savoring the moment that would change her life. The young girls of Edgar Road will have no such barriers in their path.

Back to the rest of the Van Dyke family. Daughter Gretchen didn't do too badly that weekend either. On Sunday of that weekend she ran the Capitol City Half Marathon in Olympia, Washington, running 1:35 and finishing second in her age group and eighth overall. The only member of the family who didn't run that weekend was Gretchen's husband Dave, who was training for the Newport, Oregon, marathon, so he did a long run while Gretchen ran her race. On May 30 he ran the marathon in 2:57. All in all it was a great weekend for Team Van Dyke.

June 2009

Dancing Man or Two Weeks on Vashon Island

This past summer we spent two weeks on Vashon Island, Washington, as we have done for the past several years. Vashon Island is an island about the size of Manhattan located in Puget Sound between Tacoma on the south and Seattle on the north. When you look at the island on a map the shape resembles that  of a man dancing, hence the name "Dancing Man." Following are three short running reminiscences of our stay on the island.

Chasing Gertie Though the Woods at Point Defiance

Point Defiance is a short ferry ride from Tahlequah on the

south end of Vashon Island. Point Defiance is a large peninsula jutting out into Puget Sound. It is an enormous park, with a zoo, a Japanese garden and, most important for runners, a system of trails up, down and around through dense forests of enormous fir trees stretching to reach the sky. A paved road five miles long circumnavigates the park, and I have often run that road with my daughter Gretchen when we visit. Even though we are only a few miles from downtown Tacoma, when we run at the park we feel like we are in a national forest, with very little light penetrating the dense forest. The run is not for the faint of heart though, because the road rises and falls several hundred feet between the start and the finish.

Gretchen and her group of running/triathlon friends often run in the park, but they prefer the trails through the woods over the paved road. One Saturday, while we were on the island, she invited me to take the ferry to Point Defiance to run with her friends, as I have often done in the past. In recent years I have had trouble keeping up with Gretchen when we run together, particularly when we run on hilly terrain. She glides up the hills and I slog up, sometimes stopping at the crest to regroup. But I always love the opportunity to run with Gretchen and her friends.

What I should tell you, though, not only is Gretchen a very accomplished runner, but one of her friends, Nancy Abraham,

 is also an accomplished runner and triathlete. She often finishes first in her age group (50-54) in local races. In 2007 she finished third in the 2007 world triathlon championships in the non-professional division in Lorient, France. She and Gretchen often train together, leading the other runners on their treks through the Point Defiance forest trails.

I knew what was coming when we started our run in the meadow area

at the south end of Point Defiance, but somehow I thought I was in good shape this year so maybe I could keep up with them for a while. The day was insufferably hot for the northwest, with temperatures over 90 degrees. Right from the start I was having a hard time keeping pace with Gretchen and Nancy, but once we reached the woods it was over as they continued to run easily up and down the paths through the trees. Every time I reached a small incline or rise I struggled as they continued to pull ahead. Occasionally they would stop to wait for me and offer me water, but then they would resume their persistent pace as I lagged further and further behind chasing the two of them through the woods.

After a few miles of this, Gretchen waited for me, and we moved to the paved road and shortened the run a bit to make it easier for me. We finished together after running about five miles, but Nancy continued through the woods finishing a few minutes after us, but covering much more ground than we had. The memory that sticks in my mind from that run is seeing the two of them from the back as they glided effortlessly across the forest floor, up hills then down again on the path, getting further and further ahead.

What's Wrong with This Picture?

What's wrong with this picture? Just a picture of running shoes, you say. But look closer. There is an impostor in that group, a pair that doesn't belong. What pair is that you say? Why it's the Nikes, of course—the only pair that aren't Asics.

The picture shows our family's running shoes and they all used to be Asics, until this year. For the past 30 or more years I have run in Asics, and our son Garrett and daughter Gretchen continued the legacy. When our new son-in-law joined the family, he too continued the tradition. Until this year, that is. But then he heard the siren call of Nike this summer and bought a pair of LunarGlides, which you see in the picture. It was a shock at first, to see him running in them, but they certainly looked cool with the bright orange soles, and the white Nike swoosh on the side. They just didn't fit in.

But he must have seen something in those shoes, though, that I didn't, because he set a personal best of 17:48 in a 5k race that summer, and later in the fall he set a personal best of 2:53 in the Portland marathon.

Dave, it is okay. You can still be part of our family, even wearing the Nikes. Just don't expect us to follow suit—unless, of course, you can guarantee we'll run personal bests too.

Pasta Dash

While on the island we decided to run the Pasta Dash, a 5k/10k road race in Olympia, Washington, 30 miles south of Tacoma. Seemed like a good idea at the time. Even though it was early August, we were in the northwest, and the race was late in the day, so one would think the temperatures would be ideal, especially in Olympia with sea breezes from Puget Sound cooling the air. Think again. This was not your usual summer in Seattle. While we were on Vashon Island temperatures in nearby Seattle reached a scorching, unheard of 104 degrees—a record high. We had already entered the race, so there was no turning back.

Son-in-law Dave was the smart one. He decided to run the 5k, while Gretchen and I signed up for the 10k.

The race started off on a very flat section of East Bay Drive along Budd Inlet. The 5k turned around just before a local park, Priest Point Park. I started off easy in deference to the heat, and by the first mile Gretchen was out of sight. Before we reached the 5k turnaround point, we spotted Dave already on his way back to the finish, looking strong and solid in his new Nike LunarGlides. He had clearly made the right decision to run the 5k. It was shorter, and on this hot day that mattered, of course, but even more, his course was flat—flat as the proverbially pancake. Unfortunately for me and Gretchen the race entered the hilly part of the course in Priest Point Park just after the 5k turnaround. It was lovely in the woods, but the hills were difficult, especially for an Illinois flatlander.

 The heat only made it worse. I struggled to focus, trudging up the hills, and then down again. Once we got back on the flat part of the course, the heat and the hills had taken their toll on my body, and I plodded slowly to the finish in 50:22, five minutes behind Gretchen. We had both run our worst 10k in years. Even so, Gretchen won her age group, and I won mine, although I was the only one in the over 65 age group.

Dave, on the other hand had thrived, even in the heat. Must be something about the shoes, because he had set a personal record of 17:49. He'll never go back to wearing Asics shoes again. He's now a confirmed Nike runner.

November 2009

Running in the Land of Enchantment—or What Goes Up Must Come Down

This past February Johna and I went to New Mexico to visit some friends near Santa Fe and Albuquerque to get away from the gray Midwest for a little sunshine. We had been there twice before  and loved the landscape, which is so very different from the flat Midwestern landscape we inhabit. While on the trip I managed to run every other day, which is what I usually do. Below is a recollection of the running part of the trip.

Galisteo—Elevation 6000 Feet above Sea Level
      Six miles per hour outbound/Seven miles per hour inbound

Galisteo is a small town—population 300—located about 25 miles south of Santa Fe. Our friends, Wayne and Barb King, have a lovely hacienda-ette there, with a pottery studio, stable for their two horses  and a suite attached to the studio that is perfect for the many guests who visit them from Wisconsin, where they grew up, and Ipswich, Massachusetts, which was their home prior to moving to Galisteo. They lead an interesting life there. They both are on the volunteer fire department, and Wayne is actually a Fire Captain. Wayne also has become an accomplished rider and cowboy, helping out local ranchers herding their cattle, and Barb is an accomplished potter and artist.

Galisteo is located on New Mexico Highway 41 at 6,000 feet above sea level. The highway passes within a few hundred yards of Wayne and Barb's place, but there is very little traffic. The road goes through the town, past an ancient church, Iglesia Nuestra Señora de los Remedios, and a dance hall, before proceeding north about six miles farther to the junction with US Highway 285.

I wanted to run, but wasn't sure where to run. There really weren't a lot of options. When we had visited three years before in March, I had taken a road leading out of town toward the old mining town of Madrid, but my recollection of that run was the many hills along the way, including a steep incline out of Galisteo. The safer bet seemed to be to take Highway 41 north from mile post 56 as far as seemed comfortable, so that is what I decided to do.

I ran out of the compound down the muddy road to Highway 41 feeling very sluggish and just beginning to warm up. I should note that in an effort to slow traffic coming through town, the state has recently installed solar-powered speed indicators on 41.

As I passed the one on the south end of town, just before crossing the Galisteo River, I was surprised to see my speed had registered on the sign. Six miles an hour! I surely wasn't speeding, was I? More like plodding through town.

The elevation gradually rose, but slowly enough that I didn't feel like I was exerting myself, at least on the first day. I made it near milepost 60, before turning around to get back before dark. The run back was much easier than the run out—I was sailing now that the elevation was dropping instead of climbing. When I reached the north end of town the speed sign lit up with my

pace—7 miles an hour. Clearly I was much faster at the end of my run, going downhill, than I was at the beginning. I reached my destination just after dark feeling the good tired from an exhilarating run. Later I found out that the elevation had risen to about 6,300 feet at the turnaround.

The next two times I ran in Galisteo I took the same route—each time going to milepost 60, but I could never duplicate that first day's run. I spent the next two runs plodding up the hill out of town and not running much faster on the way back. I didn't even have the courage to run by the speed sign on the way back to see how slowly I was running, but the one going out registered the same six miles per hour.

Taos—Elevation 7,200 Feet above Sea Level

Taos is a town we are in love with. The setting is fantastic, nestled in the Sangre de Cristo mountain range. Artists have been visiting and calling Taos home since the early part of the 20th century, including Willa Cather, D.H. Lawrence, Ansel Adams, and so many more. We stayed at the Mabel Dodge Luhan House, a bed and breakfast that was originally a salon of sorts and refuge for artists hosted by Mable Dodge Luhan, an arts patron and supporter.

I only did one run while we were in Taos, but once again it was up out of town and down on the way back. The run started out at about 7,200 feet and rose to 7,500 feet by the time I turned around at about four miles out of town. This run went a bit better than the last run in Galisteo, but at the end I began looking forward to going to our next destination— Albuquerque—where the elevation fell to 5,000 feet. I was looking forward to running at a lower altitude.

Albuquerque—Elevation 5,000 Feet above Sea Level

Albuquerque may be lower in altitude than Galisteo or Taos, but the run there wasn't any easier. Our friend Raye Baldwin lives in a townhouse complex on Osuna Boulevard just across from Arroyo Oso Golf Course. I was looking forward to a run along Osuna with a running/hiking trail alongside the road for several miles, but when I began my run things didn't go as planned. Instead of floating along at the lower altitude as I had expected, I was once again plodding along, even stopping from time to time. I hadn't expected that, but I continued to forge ahead anyway, eventually cutting my run short and turning around at the 2.5 mile instead of the four plus miles I had planned. But after turning around, everything made sense. I looked back down a very long incline. I had been running uphill the entire way—over 300 feet in fact. No wonder I was going so slowly! I was glad to turn around and run downhill going back to Raye's house. Happy too, to be going back to the flatlands of Evanston, wondering if any of the altitude training would improve my running performances later this year.

The Rest of the Trip

When I wasn't running, which was most of the time, we traveled all over northern New Mexico visiting art galleries, museums, historical sites and small towns and villages. Our friends Wayne and Barbara were fabulous hosts, always keeping on the move with something to see or do. We even took a chilies rellenos

cooking class in Santa Fe. Who knew pickled jalapeno peppers could taste so good.

The dry arid climate of the southwest is heaven for cars and trucks, which go on forever, without the debilitating effects of salt and rust. A local Santa Fe artist, Barbara Bowles, takes photos of ancient pickup trucks that dot the landscape. Shown with this article is one of her images, blown up, and mounted on a panel as part of an exhibit at the New Mexico History Museum in the historic Palace of the Governors with the two of us enjoying the ride to nowhere.

All in all, a great trip through the Land of Enchantment.

February 2010

The Joy of Running

My son Garrett recently e-mailed me a photograph of our 10-year old grandson Jack running chasing a soccer ball through the grass. When I first saw the photo it touched something deep inside, seeing the pure joy he exuded as he chased the ball. He's looking over at his Dad as if to say, "What are you doing, dad?" But there is more than that. There is the pure unadulterated exuberance in the long stride of his skinny legs as he glides over the turf. He is in the moment, enjoying himself. He's not running for fitness, for a medal, or to beat someone else. He's running for joy and for the sheer pleasure it brings.

Who of us cannot relate to that picture, to the time when we ran with carefree abandon? Don't you too have a memory of being a 10-year-old on the school grounds, running, maybe chasing someone, or being chased, or just running because it felt good? I know I do. I remember playing "boys chase the girls" and loving the feeling of running, being chased or chasing, sprinting fast to catch up to a classmate or to avoid being caught.

It's good for each of us to remember that time in our lives when we too ran not to race, not to beat someone, or to finish high in our age group, or to run a personal record (PR). We run for that, but at least for me, I run to experience that exuberance and joy in body loping over the grass with no particular purpose or destination.

Consuella Moore, winner of the 200 meters at the U.S. National Championship track and field meet this year, had lost the joy in her running, but had it rekindled when she remembered what had first drawn her to the sport as a youngster. Or as she said, "I look at track as a giant playground for adults, with all the events going on. One day I said, 'I really miss playing with my friends.' I had a lot of stuff going on in the past when I was running. I found out it doesn't have to be stressful. It's just like racing to the mailbox back in the day." That's what we runners need to remember and rekindle when we feel stale.

I have a few running photographs on the inside of my medicine cabinet that inspire me. One is of the national NCAA cross country meet many, many years ago. In it Steve Prefontaine of the University of Oregon and Garry Bjorkland of the University of Minnesota are running intently, but effortlessly, over the grass in a classic running duel. They are competing, but they exhibit the same joy in their effort that my grandson has. They are kids again. Another photo shows Lynn Jennings, three-time world cross country champion and 1992 bronze medalist in the 10,000 meters, winning a race with a determined look on her face. These photos provide me with the inspiration of graceful determined runners. But now I have added the picture of Jack to my medicine cabinet gallery to remind me why I love running. It too will provide me with inspiration.

August 2010

Old School

What exactly is "Old School" anyway? I believe it was one of my grown children who called me "Old School" when they laughed at my collection of cotton tee shirts that I wear when running. They have taken to giving me new technical shirts and gear made with miracle fibers that wick the sweat away from your body to replace the cotton tee shirts that usually become soaked with sweat when I run. Those cotton tee shirts and other gear have stood by me for almost 50 years, but somehow my children thought I needed to be introduced to new ways of thinking and doing. As I thought about it I realized I am an "Old School" runner in many more ways than just my running attire, and that today's runners do it much differently than I have done. They carry water bottles when they run, they use gels to get nutrition when they run marathons, they wear heart rate monitors so they know precisely their every heart palpitation during their runs and they track their workouts on the computer after they are finished. So what are some of the things that make me "Old School"?

I don't listen to music while I run. Don't get me wrong, I love my iPod, but I would never use it while I run. To me, part of the experience of running is being aware of my surroundings, listening to the sounds around me, seeing what is going on, listening to my body as the tempo of the run changes from slow to fast and back again. I get into my own zone when I run and don't need the music to distract me. I like listening to the sound of my feet slapping against the pavement, or the crunching underneath when the surface changes to crushed stone or gravel. I especially like the silence and muffled sound of my feet when running through a newly fallen snow. Would I hear those sounds with earphones on and my iPod playing? I doubt it.

What's a GU anyway? I never heard of GU until someone mentioned them to me recently. Who knew? I still remember my first Boston Marathon when the only nutrition on the course was the orange slices handed out by eager children as we trudged up Heartbreak Hill. Now you can get your GU gel in multiple flavors—Chocolate Outrage, Strawberry Banana, Mandarin Orange and Cherry Lime to name just a few. My daughter swears by them when she runs marathons or does triathlons. Time to teach an old dog new tricks? We'll see.

I ran barefoot 50 years ago. The latest running fad is barefoot running, or minimal shoes mimicking barefoot running. Have you seen the shoes we ran on in the 1970s? Those were minimal shoes. The blue Tiger shoes I ran in had a very thin sole and no heel padding and nothing to stabilize your foot, but they worked very well. As to barefoot running—I ran several college cross country races in my bare feet, not because I thought it was good for me, but because it was the ultimate elemental statement. Besides I thought it connected me in some way to a Native American incarnation of my being. Speaking of shoes, I ran my first marathon in Chuck Taylor Converse All-Star low cut gym shoes that were made for playing basketball. Now that's "Old School."

I watched Frank Shorter win the 1972 Olympic Marathon on television. All of us "Old School" guys and gals (there aren't many of those) remember vividly Frank Shorter making the bold move to the lead through the winding park path in Munich, a lead he never relinquished to become the gold medal winner, and a role model for many of us. It's as vivid as the picture 1984 picture of Joan Benoit boldly dashing to the lead in Los Angeles Summer Olympics to take the gold medal in the first women's Olympic marathon.

I have never run on a treadmill. All my running is done outside no matter what the weather—through pouring rain, snowstorms and the heat of summer—I slog on. I almost succumbed to the treadmill twice, but somehow it wasn't meant to be. Several years ago on a very, very hot day in Chicago I was going to run indoors on a treadmill at our local health club with my daughter, but it just didn't happen. Then this past year I had a project that took me to Abu Dhabi in the middle of the summer where the temperature reached 115 degrees Fahrenheit. Now that's hot, and it isn't a dry heat either, it is hot and humid, making it virtually impossible to run outdoors. I packed my running gear thinking I might run on the hotel treadmill since I would be there for a week, and didn't want to miss an entire week of running. But when I went to the hotel health spa and looked at the treadmill I couldn't bring myself to use the equipment. I was intimidated by the technology and had visions of myself falling and being shot off the belt onto the floor, looking very foolish. My streak continued! No indoor treadmill running for me.

I don't have a heart rate monitor or a Garmin. Most days I run how I feel and I think I can probably tell within 15 seconds per mile how fast I am going and whether I am going a 7:30 pace or a nine-minute per mile pace. I'm not very obsessive about my times or my pace any more, and I track the distances on the USATF web site so I know how far I have run. I can also judge when I am running too fast, or when I'm going slowly, so no heart rate monitor for me.

I ran many of my track races on a cinder track. Before there were all weather composition running tracks we ran on tracks made with cinders. Running on them was an adventure, especially if the event you were running was late in the track meet and the inside lane was indented and pocked from the previous races. Not to mention the puddles when it rained. Plus the track was measured in yards, not meters. One lap was 440 yards, not 400 meters like it is on most tracks today. A mile was four laps around, not 1,600 meters, which is slightly shy of a mile, and eight laps was two miles, not 3,200 meters, which is what it is on a metric track.

I don't carry a water bottle with me when I run. I thought a Camelback was something only a camel had, not something that I would strap on my back. I know hydration is important, but do you really need to carry a water bottle on a five or six mile run? I have seen young women jogging holding quart sized water filled bottles, and wonder why they need to carry such large containers with them. On long runs in my day we would stop at water fountains to hydrate, and on most runs of 12 miles or less, we wouldn't feel the need to drink during the run. What has changed here? I am not sure, but I can't envision myself running with a water bottle, let alone carrying water on my back as I run. I do make sure I hydrate after my runs though by drinking lots of lime Gatorade, which is just about the only liquid I do ingest.

What's a bib belt? Safety pins I know and use them to pin my race number on my singlet, but Leslie at work told me about a belt that you use to attach your number to, instead of using pins. Plus they have belts that you can attach your goos and gels to as well for easy access during the race. Who creates this stuff anyway? I guess someone who stuck themselves with the pins one time too many as they attached their number to their shirt. Me, I'll stick with safety pins.

To me running is the quintessential simple sport. Put on a pair of running shoes, a pair of socks, shorts and a cotton tee shirt and run, putting one foot down and then the other. Nothing could be more elemental. Is all this gear and emphasis on technology necessary, or is it just a way to sell more stuff to runners? I don't know, but I will be happy to continue my "Old School" ways, with occasional forays into the world of running gear my children, and now son-in-law, introduce me to.

May 2010

I Love My Physical Therapist

"**D**o you stretch before you run?", she asked. "No," I answered. "Do you stretch after you run?" Again the answer was, "No." Those were the questions Amy Terpstra asked me when I first came to her for physical therapy treatment for the tightness and pain in my right hamstring that was severely hampering my running last winter and early spring. I have been running for almost 50 years and never felt the need to stretch, either before or after my runs, so I felt a bit embarrassed answering the questions as I did, especially responding to a physical therapist like Amy.

I had been experiencing pain in my hamstring for quite some time. I tend to ignore such minor aches and pains, and usually they go away by themselves, but this pain persisted and kept getting worse. So bad that at times my right leg seemed to go out from under me and even though it would get a bit better as I warmed up, it was definitely not going away and the pain was making it very difficult to run. I finally realized it wouldn't go away by itself and I needed to do something about it, so I decided to go to my physician, even though I wasn't sure what she could do about it.

I met with my primary care physician and she interviewed me and asked about my condition. After a brief interview and recounting of my symptoms she recommended a course of physical therapy. I had not had any physical therapy treatment for any injury before and was somewhat skeptical of its ability to help me, but I was getting desperate and wanted to be able to run again without pain and discomfort.

I didn't know what to expect when I went to my first session with Amy, but I told her about my injury and that I had been running more than 40 years. That's when I made my confession. I am not sure what she thought, but I can imagine, seeing an ancient marathoner who could barely bend down to touch his knees. The first thing she did was have me lay on my back on the padded table in the curtained cubicle. She then lifted my legs, first one and then the other, and stretched them gently, first to one side and then the other. I could feel my hamstring tighten and pull as she moved my leg. It hurt. She then had me do a few more exercises that seemed to be focused on my quads, and not my hamstrings. I grabbed one of my ankles and pulled my leg to my buttocks for 30 seconds and then repeated it with the other one. We did other similar exercises, including standing on one leg on a step and then bending on that leg and touching my other foot to the ground. My session ended in 30 minutes with my quads and hamstrings both sore. Amy gave me a series of exercises to do at home before my next session.

At first nothing happened. I did the exercises, went to physical therapy sessions one or two times a week and still the pain persisted. I got new exercises for my regimen, including side lunges, which took me a bit of time to master, and walking backwards with a large rubber inner tube connecting my two legs to provide some resistance. But gradually the pain began to ease and my range of motion increased. I could tell the therapy was working even though my hamstring hurt after every therapy session as Amy stretched my leg back and forth and from side to side at the beginning of the session and then had me go though the other exercises one by one for the remainder of the half hour. I continued to do the exercises at home, but not before or after my run. So I still couldn't answer yes to the question Amy first asked me.

Finally we got to the point where the tightness and pain had diminished almost completely and I ended my round of therapy. My hamstring still isn't 100%, but it is much better and I run pain free with only minor twinges. I could tell the difference when I ran several 5k races during the spring finishing in the top one or two in my age group, but more importantly having the range of motion needed to fully utilize my conditioning and speed. I do the exercises occasionally, but not as much as when I was in therapy. I still don't stretch before or after my runs, but I am planning to begin yoga classes in 2011 as a way to continue the stretching regimen. I am grateful to Amy for helping me through this injury even though I still can't quite get myself to stretch just before, or after my run as most of my running companions do.

July 2010

Long Distance: A Year of Living Strenuously
By Bill McKinnon

Last winter, tucked away at Frank Lloyd Wright's Seth Peterson Cottage on Mirror Lake in Delton, Wisconsin, I read *Long Distance: A Year of Living Strenuously* by Bill McKinnon. It was the extremely engaging story of Bill McKinnon's yearlong quest to become an athlete. Bill McKinnon is a 37-year-old writer who had never been a serious athlete, but who wanted to challenge himself physically and mentally, so he decided to spend a year of his life training to become a cross country skier. He hired a coach and embarked on a serious training program of running and weight training and learning the skiing technique. It's a story many Evanston

Running Club members will enjoy, both those new to the sport of long distance running and those who are experienced runners.

He talks about learning the arcane language of training, of wearing a heart monitor strapped to his body and running for two or three hours trying to keep his heart rate between 135 and 140 beats per minute. He goes to the Olympic Training Center to have his fitness monitored and his body fat and VO2 measured, describing in detail the obsessions of a long-distance athlete. Slowly he transforms himself from a not very fit person, into an extremely fit athlete able to race and ski. He also discusses in detail the scientific basis of training for long-distance sports like running and cross country skiing, giving a history of the science of athletic training and how it has evolved. I found that part fascinating, especially the history of long-distance running.

Cross country skiing is an arcane sport, with much emphasis on choosing the right wax to match the snow conditions, and what happens when they don't match. There's also the importance of technique. Not only did Bill need to become running fit, he also needed to master the technique of using the skis and the poles. Then of course there is the issue of snow, longing for it to come, and what happens when it doesn't.

But about two-thirds of the way through the book the story takes a different twist when the author discovers that his 68-year-old father has been diagnosed with a brain tumor. As Bill becomes more fit and in control, his father loses control and he must deal with those two conflicting realities, taking care of his own body while he trains, and taking care of his father as he loses control of his body. That part of the story puts his quest in focus.

It's a book probably read best on a snowy winter weekend, snuggled up by a roaring fire, but I heartily recommend it to all ERC members, whether you care about cross country skiing or not.

July 2001

Bowerman and the Men of Oregon: The Story of Oregon's Legendary Coach and Nike's Co-founder
By Kenny Moore

Or as I like to call it—*Lemon and Green-—The Story of Bill Bowerman*. Lemon and green. Those are the colors of the University of Oregon Ducks from Eugene, Oregon. Just to say the words Eugene, Oregon conjures up images of running to me. I've never been there, but in my mind I have run miles on the wood chip trail dedicated to the memory of Steve Prefontaine. I have run on the wood chip trail around the stadium in Helsinki, Finland, home to that great Finnish runner, Paavo Nurmi, who is immortalized with a bronze (nude) statue just outside the stadium, but never in Eugene. The lemon and green singlet has been worn by countless distance running legends and Olympians who were coached by Bill Bowerman, former track and cross country coach at Oregon.

- Bill Dellinger—5,000 meter silver medalist—1964 Tokyo Olympics and former Oregon track coach
- Steve Prefontaine—5,000 meter silver medalist—1972 Tokyo Olympics
- Phil Knight—half-miler and founder of Nike
- Jim Grelle-—Olympian and US mile record holder in 1965, broken by Jim Ryan that same year
- Dyrol Burleson—Olympian and US mile record holder in 1961 and 1962

The list also includes Kenny Moore—two time Olympian-— fourth in the 1972 Munich Olympics. He is also a gifted writer and former senior writer for *Sports Illustrated*. I still have in my files one of the first articles he wrote for that magazine, titled *One of the Pleasures of My Life*, written I believe in 1971. In that article Moore waxes eloquent about cross country running, recalling in particular the course at the University of Kansas in Lawrence. He wrote about one particularly difficult hill near the end of the race, "Anoxia has burned every tendril of that slope's crabgrass into thousands of collegiate memories." It is that gift for writing and telling a story that Moore brings to the biography of his beloved coach, Bill Bowerman.

The book he wrote is the story of Bill Bowerman, but it is so much more. It is also the history of the running boom that began in this country in the mid-1960s and continues today. Bill Bowerman was there creating and shaping much of that history. He was influential in so many ways. As head coach at Oregon University he coached countless sub-four-minute milers and Olympians. His athletes won four NCAA track and field championships, set 13 world records and 22 American records. One of his athletes was Phil Knight, who went on to start the company that eventually became Nike. Bill was there at the beginning, and continued for many years making prototype shoes for Nike, using his athletes as guinea pigs. One particularly ill-fated project had him using tanned cod (fish) skins for uppers for a pair of shoes, reasoning that they would be perfect on a wet track repelling water. Unfortunately the shoes soaked up water, and shoes that had begun as a size nine at the beginning of the race expanded to size 12 by the end of it. He also invented the waffle shoe in 1972, a shoe I have worn on some of my fastest marathon races.

Bill Bowerman also contributed to the fitness and running boom in the 1960s. In 1966 he published a pamphlet simply titled *Jogging,* which went on to sell one million copies. He in turn was strongly influenced by Arthur Lydiard, himself a famed New Zealand Olympic coach, who also developed an exercise program for cardiac patients in his own country, reasoning that the heart is a muscle, and as such it would benefit from training. Bowerman met Lydiard on a trip to New Zealand with the world-record mile relay team. While there he lost 10 pounds after jogging daily with groups of ordinary citizens enrolled in the Lydiard's program after first being barely able to run 400 yards as an out-of-shape 50 year old. He became convinced of the benefits of regular cardiovascular exercise.

Upon returning to the United States Bowerman invited anyone of any age to come to the Hayward Field practice track to walk and jog. He did this at a time when it was thought that physical activity was only for the young and those in school. After college there were few if any programs for athletes and non-athletes alike. Or as Moore writes, "It may be hard for anyone born after 1960 to believe, but runners in those days were regarded as eccentric at best, subversive and dangerous at worst." I still remember running through a park in Stockholm, Sweden, in 1972, and listening to a group of young Swedes yelling pejoratively, "Finni, Finni," as if the only person daffy enough to be running would be a Finn, and not one of them.

Kenny Moore has written an excellent book that I heartily recommend to anyone interested in the history of our sport, the emergence of Nike and the story of Steve Prefontaine and other Oregon runners. I found the first few chapters of the book documenting his family history tedious, but the rest of the book fascinating with its recounting of the stories of the "Men of Oregon."

July 2007

Running with the Buffalos—A Season Inside with Mark Wetmore, Adam Goucher and the University of Colorado Men's Cross Country Team
By Chris Lear

This past Christmas I received a copy of *Running with the Buffalos* from my daughter Gretchen and her boyfriend Dave, our soon to be son-in-law. It was perfect timing. Just after Christmas our entire family went to Williams Bay, Wisconsin to stay in a house we were renting for a few days, because our small condominium cannot accommodate our growing family anymore, especially our son's family with two young grandsons who need space to run and jump. Two days after we arrived it started to snow, which was a delight to everyone. We were snowed in. We didn't have anywhere to go, so we could just enjoy watching the snow, as it fell throughout the day, creating a winter wonderland, with snow on all the tree branches outside our windows.

The house is one of several in a compound that are mostly on high ground overlooking a tree-filled glen that gradually slopes to the shore of Lake Geneva. Our house has a lovely bay with windows overlooking the glen, with a perfect sledding slope right out the door. So while everyone else cavorted in the snow, sledding and making snow forts, I sat in the bay reading my new book with relish, occasionally looking out the window to survey the scene as children, young and old, went down the hill and over a makeshift jump screaming wildly with delight.

Running with the Buffalos is the story of a single season with the University of Colorado men's cross country team. The year is 1998. The team was led by Adam Goucher, a very talented runner, now perhaps better known as the husband of Kara Goucher, who finished 3rd in the World Track and Field Championship 10k in Osaka, Japan. The team was coached by Mark Wetmore, who came to CU in the fall of 1991 and began as a volunteer assistant distance coach who was later named head cross country coach of both the men's and women's teams in 1992. Wetmore is a disciple of Arthur Lydiard, the New Zealander, whose training methods became well known and emulated after three of his athletes— Peter Snell, Barry Magee and Murray Halberg—each won a medal in the 1960 Olympics in Rome. Snell won the gold medal in the 800 meters, Halberg gold in the 5,000 meters and Magee bronze in the marathon. Lydiard's methods were unique for the time, with all of his runners, from 800 meters on up, running very high mileage marathon-type training for a sustained period of time to build up their endurance, followed by a period of speed training with repetitions over shorter distances with decreasing rest between, and then followed by increased speed before a period of tapering and rest before major competitions. It is a program that forms the training foundation of our current generation of runners. Wetmore used Lydiard's methods to build a strong cross country tradition at CU, culminating in first-place finishes by the men's team in 2001, 2004 and 2007, and in 2000 and 2004 by the women's team. 2004 was a special year because both the men's and women's teams were NCAA cross country champions.

The book documents the team's journey from training camp in early fall, through the NCAA cross country championships in Lawrence, Kansas, in November. We see what it is like to train at a very high collegiate level. It is a season with the normal trials and tribulations of hard training, including injuries, disappointments as the athletes try to make the final cut of seven runners who will run in the championship races later in the season, and even an unexpected tragedy. We follow the team as they do their long, hard aerobic training on trails and routes that Mark Wetmore personally ran and developed for the team. With its location in Boulder the runs are all done at altitude, many beginning at 7,000 feet and climbing even higher. We get to know the runs by their names.

- The Dam—A 10-mile all-out run to the five-mile mark at a dam, and back.
- Flagstaff (Mountain)—Named for a flagstaff visible from the beginning of the run, which has a 1,400-foot elevation gain before coming back.
- The Tank—Named for a large water tower at the six-mile mark.
- Mags—Magnolia Road, a 17-plus-mile route that is the location of their weekly long runs.
- Milers—These are speed work with athletes running one-mile repeats with a short rest interval between each one.

Later in the season we watch in awe at the workouts as the speed increases and intervals between their repetitions get shorter and shorter, sharpening and honing their well-tuned running machines for the championship races.

It took a bit of time for me to get into the book, especially since Adam Goucher was the only runner on the team I had ever heard of. But I found about midway that I was hooked, wondering how the team was going to do. Would they overcome their adversities and injuries? Would Adam Goucher win the NCAA championship he was training so hard to achieve? Would the team be able to overcome their main rivals, the University of Arkansas and Stanford University, and be crowned the team champion?

Needless to say, I enjoyed the book and recommend it to my running friends. I only wish there would have been more photographs of the runners and the team interspersed throughout the text.

January 2008

16810339R00083

Made in the USA
Charleston, SC
11 January 2013